9-45
DU
07/09

CRIMINAL LAW
IN A
NUTSHELL

AUSTRALIA
Law Book Company
Sydney

CANADA and USA
Carswell
Toronto

HONG KONG
Sweet & Maxwell Asia

NEW ZEALAND
Brookers
Wellington

SINGAPORE and MALAYSIA
Sweet & Maxwell Asia
Singapore

NUTSHELLS

CRIMINAL LAW
IN A
NUTSHELL

EIGHTH EDITION

by

PAUL DOBSON, LL.B., Barrister of Lincoln's Inn

London • Sweet & Maxwell • 2008

Published in 2008 by Sweet & Maxwell Limited of
100 Avenue Road, London, NW3 3PF
Typeset by LBJ Typesetting Ltd of Kingsclere
Printed in Great Britain by Creative Print and Design Group

No natural forests were destroyed to make this product.
Only farmed timber was used and replanted.

A CIP catalogue record for this book is available
from the British Library.

ISBN 978–1–8470–3123–5

©
Sweet & Maxwell
2008

PREFACE

This edition includes coverage of substantial developments in both statute law and case law, as well as coverage of recent proposals for reform of the law.

Since the last edition, new cases include significant decisions on key issues at the highest level: in the House of Lords, *Hasan* (on duress), *Kennedy* (on manslaughter) and *Saik* (on conspiracy); in the Court of Appeal, *Heard* (on specific/basic intent) and *Barnes* (on consent); in the Privy Council, *Holley* (on provocation) and *Wheatley* (on theft/dishonesty). All these and other recent decisions are included in this edition.

New legislation has caused considerable changes in this edition. The expanding law of homicide means that this edition includes coverage of the new statutory offence of corporate manslaughter (enacted in the Corporate Manslaughter and Corporate Homicide Act 2007) as well as coverage of the statutory offence (enacted in the Domestic Violence, Crime and Victims Act 2004) of causing or allowing the death of a child or a vulnerable adult. Meanwhile, the repeal of a whole range of deception offences in the Theft Acts 1968 and 1978 and their replacement by fraud and other offences in the Fraud Act 2006 has meant a complete re-write of Chapter 10 to include coverage of this new law. The sample Examination Guidance Questions in the final chapter have been thoroughly revised to relate to the law as it now is.

Finally, the practice has been continued of including, usually at the end of relevant chapters, a note on possible reform of the law. In this edition these notes now include coverage of three recent Law Commission Reports on: *Inchoate Liability for Assisting and Encouraging Crime; Participation in Crime; Murder, Manslaughter and Infanticide.*

I hope that this edition will be a valuable support to students as they prepare for their examinations in this most fascinating of subjects.

Paul Dobson
Woodford Green
January 2008

CONTENTS

1. *ACTUS REUS*

A person cannot ordinarily be found guilty of a serious criminal offence unless two elements are present: the *actus reus* or guilty act and the *mens rea* or guilty mind. A wrongful act on its own therefore cannot usually be criminal unless the wrongful state of mind required for that offence is also present.

1. WHAT IS AN *ACTUS REUS*?

An *actus reus* consists of more than just an act. It includes whatever circumstances and consequences are required for liability for the offence in question, i.e. all the elements of an offence other than the mental element.

Some crimes, such as murder and criminal damage, require the production of consequences or results. Others, such as theft and rape, merely require a course of conduct.

If any element of the *actus reus* is missing then there is no liability.

Authority: *Deller* (1952). D had made what he thought was a false representation in order to sell his car. In fact the representation was true. He was charged under the Larceny Act 1916 with obtaining property (the purchase price) by false pretences. One part of the *actus reus*, the circumstance that the representation he made was false, was missing. Therefore there was no liability. The fact that this was purely accidental was irrelevant. (On the law as it is today he would, however, be guilty of attempting to commit the offence—see Ch.5.)

2. VOLUNTARY CONDUCT

The accused's conduct must be "voluntary" if he is to incur liability. It may be involuntary for a variety of reasons.

Automatism

This is considered in more detail as a defence in Ch.6. Automatism occurs when D performs a physical act or acts but is unaware of what he is doing, or is not in control of his actions.

Judges have defined automatism in various ways including "acts performed involuntarily", "unconscious involuntary action", and "involuntary movement of the . . . limbs of a person".

Automatism can be seen as relevant to *actus reus* in that the act is not a voluntary act, or alternatively in terms of *mens rea* in that there is no mental element present in relation to the act because the defendant is not aware of what (s)he is doing.

Physical force

The conduct may be involuntary in that it is physically forced by someone else, in which case there will be no *actus reus*.

Reflex actions

Sometimes people can respond to something with a spontaneous reflex action over which they have no control. Although slightly different, this is sometimes classed as a form of automatism. The classic example is that given in *Hill v Baxter* (1958) of someone being stung by a swarm of bees while driving, and losing control of the car.

"State of Affairs" cases

Some unusual cases cannot be discussed in terms of voluntary acts and are often referred to as the "state of affairs" cases. These are cases where the *actus reus* consists of circumstances and sometimes consequences but no "acts", i.e. "being" rather than "doing" offences.

Authority: *Winzar v Chief Constable of Kent* (1983). D was convicted of "being found drunk in a highway contrary to s.12 of the Licensing Act 1872." This conviction was upheld on appeal despite the fact that D had been taken involuntarily to the highway by the police who had found him drunk in a hospital.

These cases incidentally present problems of *mens rea* too. What was the guilty state of mind of Winzar? (See Ch.3.)

3. CAUSATION

Questions of causation can present problems in the consideration of *actus reus*. In "result crimes" (i.e. where a consequence is part of the *actus reus*), not only must the prosecution prove a forbidden act in forbidden circumstances, but they must also prove that the defendant's conduct caused the required consequence.

This causal connection is often difficult to make. Murder is the major example of a result crime, (i.e. one where a consequence is part of the *actus reus*). There are four main problem areas.

(i)   When is the act a substantial cause of death?
(ii) Cumulative and alternative causes.
(iii) What is the legal effect of an intervening event?
(iv) What is the legal effect of negligent medical treatment?

Substantial cause of death

For liability, D's conduct need not be the sole or even the main cause of death, but it must be a substantial cause. However, this is impossible to quantify precisely. D's act must have had a significant effect, a more than minimal effect, to be an operating and substantial cause, but it is not necessary to give a jury technical instructions on this matter.

Authority: *Notman* (1994). D charged at a policeman, and the policeman tried to protect himself by tripping D. In doing so he injured his own ankle. D was liable for causing actual bodily harm because his act had more than a minimal effect on the chain of events.

In many of the cases policy reasons, although not overtly expressed, obviously influence the courts in their decisions.

Authority: *Adams* (1957). Devlin J. directed the jury that deliberately giving painkilling drugs to shorten life could constitute murder even if the patient would die in a few weeks or months anyway. He went on to say that if drugs are given to relieve pain, and an incidental consequence is the shortening of life, then there is no liability. This is not an easy distinction to make. It seems to be a policy distinction which cannot be justified in strict logic, especially as motive is deemed to be irrelevant in criminal law.

Cumulative or alternative causes

It is much easier to establish liability if the defendant's act was one of a number of causes which, cumulatively, could be said to have caused the harm, than if it is merely one possible alternative cause.

Authority: *Watson* (1989). The victim was elderly and frail. He was burgled by D. Following this, and consequent visits by police and council repairmen, he suffered a heart attack and died. Although D's conviction for manslaughter was quashed on appeal because the jury had not been properly directed on causation, it was clear that the burglary caused the visits by police and repair men, which in turn might have caused the heart attack. This could establish a causal link, a chain of causation. This situation is different from that where there are possible alternative causes. In such a case, causation is more difficult to establish.

Authority: *Armstrong* (1989). D supplied heroin and a syringe to a person who took the drug and subsequently died. Evidence showed that he had already consumed an amount of alcohol which could be fatal in itself. It was held that there was not sufficient evidence to establish whether death was caused by only one of the possible causes or by a combination of both.

Intervening events

Sometimes, after the defendant's initial act, and before the required consequence occurs, there is an intervening act or event which contributes to that consequence.

If the intervening act or event is completely unconnected with the defendant's act, was unforeseeable, and brought about the consequence on its own, then it breaks the chain of causation and the defendant incurs no liability for the consequence. If the consequence is caused by a combination of the two causes, and the defendant's act remains a significant cause, then the defendant will still be liable.

Authority: *Malcherek* (1981). D's victim was put on a life support machine as a result of the injuries D inflicted. After several days, and acting in accordance with the practice of a received body of medical opinion, doctors turned off the machine and the victim died. D was convicted of murder and appealed on the issue of causation, which he said should have been put to the jury. The appeal was dismissed. The court said that D's act was a substantial cause of death and any other contributory cause was immaterial.

If the intervening act is an act of the victim himself, then the courts ask whether the victim's response was "within a range of responses which might be anticipated". If so, it will not break the chain of causation.

Authority: *Roberts* (1971). A car driver gave a lift to a young woman. He ordered her to remove her clothes and began pulling at her coat. She opened the door and jumped out of the moving car, suffering some injuries. He appealed against his conviction for an assault occasioning actual bodily harm, claiming that he had not caused her injuries. Dismissing the appeal, the Court of Appeal held that where a victim is injured in attempting to escape from threatened violence, the test of causation is whether it was "the natural result of what the (accused) did, in the sense that it could reasonably have been foreseen as the consequence of what he was saying or doing". The chain of causation will be broken only if the victim's act is so daft or unexpected that no reasonable person could be expected to foresee it.

Authority: *Pagett* (1983). D was being pursued by armed policemen. In trying to escape, he held a girl in front of him as protection and shot at the policemen. They instinctively fired back and the girl was killed. The court held that D's act had caused the death as the intervening act had been a forseeable consequence of his action and had not broken the chain of causation.

A refusal by the victim to accept treatment is not an intervening act and it will not break the chain of causation.

Authority: *Blaue* (1975). D stabbed his victim, piercing her lung. She refused on religious grounds to accept a blood transfusion which would have saved her life. The Court of Appeal held that her refusal of treatment, whether reasonable or unreasonable, did not break the chain of causation. It was said that the accused must "take his victim as finds her", i.e. in this case, a Jehovah's Witness who would refuse treatment.

Does this same approach also apply to an intervening act by the victim? An act by the victim which is so daft as to be totally unforeseeable can, if on its own it brings about the consequence, break the chain of causation—see *Roberts* above.

Authority: *Dear* (1996). D slashed the victim several times with a sharp knife. The victim died of those wounds. D argued that the death had been caused by the victim who had committed suicide either by re-opening his wounds or, the wounds having re-opened themselves, by failing to staunch the consequent blood flow. The Court of Appeal held that the judge had correctly directed the jury in asking them to decide whether the injuries inflicted by the accused were an operating and substantial cause of the death. The court said that the niceties of the doctrine of *novus actus interveniens* and foreseeability should not invade the criminal law.

This is not in line with the approach in *Roberts*, above, and was unnecessary for the decision, since in this case the victim died of the wounds inflicted by the accused, albeit they might have been aggravated by the victim. It is thought that a totally daft, and thus unforeseeable, decision of the victim to kill himself can break the chain of causation, e.g. the victim decides to kill herself and dies of an overdose of sleeping tablets deliberately taken because she can no longer take the pain from a small finger-prick inflicted by the accused.

Negligent medical treatment

The courts are now very unwilling as a matter of policy to find that medical treatment has broken the chain of causation when it follows an initial unlawful act by someone else. The first two cases below conflict with each other. The first case has subsequently been distinguished on its own particular facts and has very little general application any longer.

Authority: *Jordan* (1956). D stabbed his victim, who died several days later after undergoing medical treatment. It was finally established on appeal that the wound had been healing well but the medical treatment was grossly negligent. The victim had unnecessarily been given an antibiotic to which he was allergic. This "palpably wrong" treatment may have been the medical cause of death. The court held that the jury might have reached a verdict of not guilty if they had had all the medical evidence, and the conviction was quashed.

Authority: *Smith* (1959). D, a soldier, stabbed another soldier, who was carried to the medical officer in charge. The medical officer was dealing with a series of emergencies and failed to appreciate the seriousness of the victim's wounds. The treatment he gave him was not beneficial and may well have made his condition worse. The victim died of his stab wounds. D was found guilty of murder and appealed. Dismissing the appeal, and distinguishing *Jordan*, the court held that D's stabbing was at the time of death an operating and substantial cause of death. The chain of causation will be broken only if the original wound is merely the setting in which another cause operates, i.e. only if the second cause is so overwhelming as to make the original wound merely part of the history.

The Court of Appeal has subsequently confirmed the approach taken in *Smith*, indicating that *Jordan* has virtually no relevance any more, except in the most "extraordinary or extreme" case.

Authority: *Cheshire* (1991). D had shot his victim. Taken to hospital, the victim contracted a respiratory infection causing a respiratory blockage. He died from the operation which was consequently given, and possibly he was negligently treated by the doctors. Dismissing D's appeal against his murder conviction, the Court of Appeal held that even where negligent treatment is the immediate cause of death, that does not break the chain of causation unless it was so independent of the accused's acts and so potent in causing the death, as to render the acts of the accused insignificant.

4. OMISSIONS

"Unless a statute specifically so provides, or . . . the common law imposes a duty upon one person to act in a particular way towards another . . . a mere omission to act (cannot lead to criminal liability)." (Miller, (1982).)

A positive duty to act exists in the following circumstances:

a) *Special relationship*

A special relationship between the defendant and the victim can create a duty. The most obvious example is parent and child, but other examples occur where people are in positions of authority or responsibility.

Authority: *Gibbins and Proctor* (1918). The first defendant was the father of a child. He, together with the second, female, defendant with whom he was living, omitted to feed the child so that it died. Their convictions for murder were upheld.

The relationships of doctor-patient can cause particular difficulties where the patient is severely handicapped. Although there is no separate rule within criminal law which exculpates doctors who do not treat these patients, it is clear that the extent of a doctor's duty in such a case is a very complex issue, and that the use of medication or extraordinary medical treatment may not be compulsory. This issue has been considered more recently in civil cases.

Authority: *Re J* (1991). This case concerned possible treatment to a severely mentally and physically handicapped five month old baby who intermittently needed to be put on a respirator in order to be kept alive. A High Court order was made (he was a ward of court) that, should it become necessary again to use a machine to keep him breathing, it was up to doctors to decide whether that was the appropriate treatment. The implication is that there is no automatic duty to keep him alive at all costs.

Authority: *Airdale N.H.S. Trust v Bland* (1993). A handicapped person in a persistent vegetative state was on a life support machine and his parents sought to have the support discontinued. The House of Lords held that it was not unlawful to withdraw artificial nutrition and hydration for such a person. It was lawful not to continue to supply the patient with care which would prolong his life.

Active termination of the patient's life, however, e.g. by lethal injection, is unlawful no matter how serious the patient's suffering. [That is so even if the patient is (a) incapable of killing herself without assistance, and (b) actively asking for that assistance: *R. (on the application of Pretty) v D.P.P.* (2001).]

Under the Mental Capacity Act 2005 (ss.24–26, a person (P) is able to make an "advance decision" stating that, if at some later stage he lacks capacity to give consent to his own medical treatment, then in the circumstances stated in his advance decision, the specified treatment (including, if the advance decision so states, life sustaining treatment,) shall not be given or shall be discontinued. That advance decision will be valid if at the relevant time: (i) P has not withdrawn it; (ii) P has not subsequently made a lasting power of attorney giving his attorneys power to consent to the relevant medical treatment;

(iii) P has not done anything inconsistent with it being his fixed decision, and; (iv) P lacks capacity to consent to medical treatment. A person (e.g. a doctor) "does not incur liability for the consequence of withholding or withdrawing a treatment from P if, at the time, he reasonably believes that an advance decision exists which is valid and applicable to the treatment" (s.26(3)).

The Act also provides for P to be able, while still of full capacity, to make a lasting power of attorney which can include giving P's attorneys power to make decisions about P's welfare if P becomes incapable of giving consent himself. This does not, however, reverse the decision in *Pretty* (above) and open the door to the attorneys giving permission for the euthanasia of P, since it does not legalise any act done which would be unlawful if P himself had consented to it.

b) Voluntary assumption of responsibility

Someone who voluntarily assumes responsibility for another person also assumes the positive duty to act reasonably for the general welfare of that person and may be liable for omissions which prove fatal.

Authority: *Gibbins and Proctor* (above). The female defendant, although not the mother of the child, had assumed responsibility by living with the father and the child.

Authority: *Stone and Dobinson* (1977). A couple had taken in an elderly aunt to live with them. They omitted to care for her properly, failing to call the doctor or medical services, with the result that she died. They were held to have assumed responsibility for her and were guilty of manslaughter.

c) Duty under a contract

A person may be under a positive duty to act because of his obligations under a contract. The duty may be to the other contracting party or to a third person.

Authority: *Pittwood* (1902). D, a railway crossing keeper, forgot to shut the gate before a train came. Someone crossing the line was struck by the train and killed. The court held that D owed a duty to all users of the crossing and not just to his employers. D was accordingly guilty of manslaughter.

d) Statutory duty

In some circumstances statute makes it a criminal offence to omit to do something. For example, s.170 of the Road Traffic Act 1988 makes it an offence, if one is involved in an accident, to omit to either report it within 24 hours to the police or to give all relevant details to any other person at the scene of the accident reasonably requesting them.

e) Duty due to defendant's prior conduct

If the defendant has acted positively although innocently to create a state of affairs which might cause damage or injury, and subsequently becomes aware of the danger he has created, there arises a duty to act reasonably to avert that danger.

Authority: *Miller* (1983). D was squatting in a house and fell asleep smoking. The mattress caught fire and he woke up. Instead of putting out the fire he moved into another room and went back to sleep. The house caught fire and the House of Lords held him liable for arson. D had unwittingly brought about a situation of danger to property. Once he realised this, he was under a self-induced duty to act positively to avert it.

This final category of liability is a fairly recent one and there may be more to come.

Proposals for reform

The Law Commission in its Report No. 218 "Offences Against the Person and General Principles" (1994), in relation to offences against the person, states that liability for omission should be limited to serious offences, namely homicide, intentional serious injury, torture, unlawful detention, kidnapping, abduction and aggravated abduction. The Law Commission also decided for the present not to try to limit common law duties to act which at present give rise to liability for omissions.

Following the Law Commission Report No. 282 "Children: Their Accidental Death or Serious Injury" (2003), urging protection for children from a foreseeable risk of death or serious injury within their own household, Parliament enacted the

Domestic Violence, Crime and Victims Act 2004 which includes the new offence of causing or allowing the death of a child or vulnerable adult (see p.117 below).

2. MENS REA

Mens rea is the culpable state of mind which is necessary, together with the *actus reus*, for a criminal offence to be committed. The *mens rea* required varies from crime to crime. There are four states of mind which separately or together can constitute the necessary *mens rea* for a criminal offence.

1. INTENTION

Intention must be distinguished from motive, which is irrelevant to liability. This distinction is not always an easy one.

Authority: *Steane* (1947). D was charged with broadcasting "with intent to assist the enemy". He had broadcast for the enemy during World War II because of threats to his family. The court held that he was not guilty because his intent was not to assist the enemy but to save his family. The student should consider this in the light of the definition of intent in terms of direct and oblique intent. One possible explanation may be that this was a very unusual case where only direct intent, i.e. desiring the consequence, was sufficient for *mens rea*.

Direct and oblique intent

Intent can be direct intent or oblique intent. Direct intent is where the consequence is desired and the accused decides to bring it about, or to do his best to do so. Oblique intent can be said to exist or be capable of existing when the accused sees the consequence as certain or virtually certain as a result of his actions and, although he does not positively desire it (he may in fact hope it does not happen), he goes ahead with his actions anyway.

There is a distinction between intention and recklessness. If the accused foresees a consequence as a likely, or a probable, or even just a possible, result of his action, and he goes ahead with his action and the consequence does indeed result, the accused can be said to have caused it recklessly. Foresight of the consequence is not, however, enough for intention. Even foresight of the consequence as highly likely to result is still not the same thing as intention. Nor must the jury be told that it is. If, however, the accused foresaw the consequence as virtually certain, that may lead the jury to conclude that the accused did have an intention to produce the consequence.

Authority: *Moloney* (1985). D and his stepfather had a shooting contest to see who could load and fire a shotgun faster. D got his gun loaded and aimed first. It was aimed at his stepfather who challenged him to fire. D did this and killed his stepfather. He was charged with murder. The direction to the jury on intention was that D had the necessary *mens rea* if he had foreseen death as a probable consequence of his actions, even if he did not desire it. The House of Lords quashed D's murder conviction, substituting a verdict of guilty of manslaughter, holding that only an intention to kill or to cause really serious injury would suffice for murder. Lord Bridge suggested guidelines which could be given to a jury to help them decide upon the issue of intention: (1) Was death or really serious injury a natural consequence of what the accused did? (2) Did the accused realise that death or really serious injury was a natural consequence of what the accused did? If the jury considered that the answer to both these questions was yes, that was not conclusive proof of intention but was something from which the jury might infer that the accused intended death or really serious injury.

Authority: *Hancock and Shankland* (1986). D and another had dropped concrete blocks onto a motorway from a bridge in order to block the road and stop a taxi which was carrying a working miner to work during a miners' strike. One block hit the taxi's windscreen and killed the driver. At the murder trial, the judge directed the jury using the guidelines given by Lord Bridge in *Moloney* (above). The House of Lords quashed the resulting convictions for murder and substituted manslaughter convictions. Their Lordships held that the *Moloney* guidelines were defective since they did not direct the jury to consider the matter of probability. The jury should be asked to consider: (1) Was death or really serious injury a natural and probable consequence of what the accused did? (2) Did the accused realise that death or really serious injury was a natural and probable consequence of what the accused did? The jury should be told that the more probable it was, the more likely it was that the accused foresaw it; and the more probable the accused realised it to be, the more likely it was that he intended it. These were guidelines which the jury could be given to help them to decide whether to draw the inference that the accused intended death or really serious injury.

Authority: *Nedrick* (1986). D had pushed lighted material through a letter box in order to frighten his victim, but in fact killed two occupants of the house. The judge directed the jury that if D realised that death was highly likely to result, then he was guilty of murder. The Court of Appeal allowed D's appeal, holding that the judge had equated foresight with intention. The judge should have made it clear that it was for the jury to decide if D had the necessary intention. Lord Lane C.J. gave a model direction:

> ". . . the jury should be directed that they are not entitled to infer the necessary intention unless they feel sure that death or serious bodily harm was a virtual certainty (barring some unforeseen intervention) as a result of the defendant's actions and that the defendant appreciated that such was the case".

Authority: *Woollin* (1998). D lost his temper and threw his three-month-old son on to a hard surface, thereby killing him. At D's trial for murder the judge directed the jury in accordance with the model direction given by Lord Lane C.J. in Nedrick. He went on, however, to say that the jury could infer the necessary intent if they were satisfied that D realised and appreciated that there was a substantial risk that he would cause serious injury. Quashing the murder conviction and substituting a conviction for manslaughter, the House of Lords held that the latter part of the direction was wrong. Their Lordships specifically upheld the correctness of the model direction suggested by Lord Lane in *Nedrick* (see above), saying that it may be appropriate to give such a direction in any case where the defendant may not have desired the result of his act. Their Lordships did suggest, however, that the word "infer" in that model direction be changed to "find" and made it clear that the guidelines given in *Hancock and Shankland* are no part of the model direction.

The model direction in *Nedrick* (as amended by their Lordships in *Woollin*) is not a definition of intention. It is merely guidance to assist a jury in determining whether the defendant had the necessary intention: *Matthews and Alleyne* (2003). Thus, if the jury finds that the defendant appreciated that death was a virtual certainty, that finding allows, but does not require, the jury to conclude that he intended death. The jury must be left in no doubt that that final issue is for them to consider and decide upon.

The model direction is probably relevant to all offences requiring proof of intention and not just murder, though in *Woollin*, Lord Steyn said that intention did not necessarily have the same meaning throughout the criminal law.

Authority: *Walker and Hayles* (1990). Ds were charged with attempted murder. They dropped their victim from a third floor balcony, severely injuring him. They had previously threatened to kill him. The Court of Appeal held that intent had the same meaning for all offences, and there was no narrower definition applicable to attempts.

Specific and basic intent

The distinction between crimes of basic intent and crimes of specific intent is important principally in relation to a defence based on voluntary intoxication and is considered in Ch.6.

2. RECKLESSNESS

Recklessness is the taking of an unjustified risk. There are various factors which are relevant in deciding whether the risk is justified and which a jury would be expected to take into account:

  (i) how likely it is that the risked consequence will occur;
 (ii) how socially useful the acts are; and
(iii) how easily precautions could be taken to avoid or mini-
      mise the risk.

"Cunningham" recklessness

The test for recklessness is subjective, i.e. the defendant must himself have realised the risk. It is not an objective test based on the standards of the reasonable man. Any liability based on those objective terms is classed as liability for negligence.

Authority: *Cunningham* (1957). D was charged under s.23 of the Offences against the Person Act 1861 with "maliciously administering a noxious thing so as to endanger life". He had broken a gas meter to steal the money in it and the gas had seeped out into the neighbouring house where the victim lived. This made her ill endangering her life. Quashing his conviction, the Court of Appeal held that the word "maliciously" did not require any wickedness but did require either intention or recklessness, the latter requiring that the accused had himself foreseen the possibility of the consequence occurring (here, that the noxious substance, gas, might be inhaled and thereby endanger life).

"Caldwell" recklessness

A much wider—and largely objective—definition of recklessness was introduced in *Caldwell*. It covered the situation where the risk of the consequence occurring would have been obvious to an ordinary person even though the accused gave no thought to the possibility.

Authority: *Caldwell* (1981). D deliberately started a fire at his victim's hotel. He was charged with intentionally or recklessly damaging property belonging to another, being reckless as to whether the life of another would be endangered thereby. He claimed that he had not realised that there was anyone in the hotel and had not realised that life would be endangered. The House of Lords held that a person was reckless as to a consequence if two requirements were satisfied: (1) the accused's actions created a risk of that consequence, a risk which would be obvious to an ordinary prudent sober person and (2) the accused either failed to give any thought to that possibility or else recognised the risk and nevertheless went ahead with his actions. According to their Lordships, this definition of recklessness applied to any modern statutory offence which included the word "reckless", "recklessness" or "recklessly".

Authority: *Elliott v C.* (1983). D was a 14-year-old girl of low intelligence who had been out all night without food or sleep. She entered a garden shed, poured out some white spirit and threw lighted matches onto it. She was charged with recklessly destroying the shed. The magistrates found that she gave no thought to the risk of that damage, and even if she had, she would not have been capable of appreciating it. The Divisional Court held that this was irrelevant to the issue of recklessness. When the court in *Caldwell* had talked about an "obvious" risk they had meant obvious to the ordinary person if he had thought about it, and not obvious to the defendant if he had thought about it.

In holding that D had been reckless, the Divisional Court loyally, though reluctantly, followed and applied the decision in *Caldwell*.

Goodbye to *Caldwell*

In the years following the decision in *Caldwell*, the courts had to decide which offences were subject to the definition of recklessness in *Cunningham* and which were subject to the *Caldwell* definition. It was held that the *Cunningham* definition applied to offences against the person: *Savage, Parmenter* (1991). It also became clear that *Caldwell* recklessness had no place in involuntary manslaughter by gross negligence: *Adomako* (1994) (see Ch.8). Nor did it have any place in the law of rape: *Satnam* (1984). *Caldwell* recklessness did apply to the statutory offences of reckless driving and causing death by reckless driving (*Lawrence*, 1981 and *Reid*, 1992). The Road Traffic Act 1991, however, replaced those two offences with the offences of dangerous driving and causing death by dangerous driving. Thus, by 2003 the *Caldwell* definition of recklessness had come to apply to only a small range of offences, probably restricted to offences of criminal damage in the Criminal Damage Act 1971 and to offences of reckless driving committed before July 1992. In 2003 *Caldwell* became a complete dead letter, when it was reversed by the House of Lords.

Authority: *R. v G and another* (2003). Two boys, aged 11 and 13, entered the back yard of a shop, put newspapers beneath wheelie bins there, and set light to the newspapers. The fire spread to the wheelie bins and then to the shop and other commercial premises, causing about £1 million worth of damage. Neither boy realised that there was any risk that the fire might spread to the buildings. They were charged under the Criminal Damage Act 1971 with recklessly damaging property belonging to another, namely the buildings. Quashing their conviction, the House of Lords held that the decision in *Caldwell* had been wrong and should be departed from. By using the word "recklessly" rather than the word "maliciously" in the Criminal Damage Act, Parliament had not intended a different meaning but was simply using a modern word. Lord Bingham said that:

> "A person acts recklessly with respect to:
> - a circumstance when he is aware of a risk that it exists or will exist;
> - a result, when he is aware of a risk that it will occur;
>
> and it is, in the circumstances known to him, unreasonable to take the risk."

That definition was taken from the Draft Criminal Code Bill annexed to the Law Commission's report entitled *A Criminal Code for England and Wales* (1989, Law Com No. 177).

The decision in *R. v G and another* was limited to the meaning of recklessness in the Criminal Damage Act 1971. However, by the time of *R. v G and Another*, it appears that *Caldwell* recklessness did not have a wider application. Thus *Caldwell* is now a matter of history. *R. v G and another* has restored the meaning of recklessness to what it was prior to *Caldwell*.

3. NEGLIGENCE

Negligence consists of a falling below the standard of the ordinary reasonable man, and either doing something he would not do, or not doing something which he would do. The test is objective, based on the hypothetical person, and not subjective, based on the defendant himself. Not all negligent behaviour is criminal. Relatively few crimes are defined in terms of negligence. The main one, manslaughter, requires gross negligence (see *Adomako*, Ch.8.). For some other crimes of negligence, see harassment (p.89 below) and causing or allowing the death of a child or vulnerable adult (p.117 below).

4. BLAMELESS INADVERTENCE

A person is blamelessly inadvertent with regard to a consequence or circumstance if he did not realise that it might exist or occur, and no reasonable person would have so realised.

Crimes in which a person with this state of mind can be found guilty are referred to as crimes of strict liability, although the situation where a person can be found guilty of a criminal offence when he is blamelessly inadvertent with regard to all the elements of the *actus reus* are rare.

5. TRANSFERRED INTENT

The defendant will be liable for an offence if he has the necessary *mens rea* and commits the *actus reus* even if the victim differs from the one intended, or the consequence occurs in a different way. An intention to cause a particular kind of harm to X can be used to justify a conviction of causing that same kind of harm to Y.

Authority: *Latimer* (1886). D aimed a blow at one person with his belt. The belt recoiled off that person and hit the victim, who was severely injured. The court held that D was liable for maliciously wounding the victim. His malice, i.e. his *mens rea*, was transferred from his intended to his unintended victim.

A limitation to the doctrine of transferred *mens rea*, however, is that an intention to cause grievous bodily harm to X cannot be used to justify a conviction of murder of Y. There must be compatibility between the crime intended and the crime charged.

Authority: *Attorney General's Reference No.3 of 1994.* D stabbed his pregnant girlfriend with intent to cause her grievous bodily harm. She died of her injuries and he pleaded guilty to her manslaughter. Subsequently the child was born alive but then died of the injuries D had inflicted. D was charged with murder of the child. The House of Lords held that the fact that at the time of the attack the child had not been born and was born later before dying of the injuries did not prevent a charge of homicide being successful. However it was not possible in law to transfer an intention to cause a particular kind of harm (grievous bodily harm) to the mother to justify conviction for a different kind of harm to the baby (murder). There had to be some compatibility between the original intention and the actual occurrence. The accused was therefore guilty not of murder but only of constructive manslaughter, since D had committed a dangerous unlawful act.

Authority: *Pembliton* (1874). D threw a stone at some people. He missed, and broke a window. He was not guilty of damaging the window as he had no *mens rea* for that offence and the *mens rea* for a completely different offence could not be transferred to make him liable.

6. COINCIDENCE OF ACTUS REUS AND MENS REA

One final problem in this area concerns the coincidence in time of the *actus reus* and the *mens rea* . The two must coincide for there to be criminal liability. The courts have developed ways of finding coincidence of *actus reus* and *mens rea* when the events take place over a period of time and constitute a course of events.

Continuing acts

One way is to say that an *actus reus* is sometimes a continuing act and a later *mens rea* can therefore coincide.

Authority:　*Fagan v Metropolitan Police Commissioner* (1969). D accidentally drove his car on to a policeman's foot and when he realised, he refused to remove it immediately. The court held that the *actus reus* of the assault was a continuing act in progress all the time the car was on the policeman's foot. So the subsequent *mens rea* could, and did, coincide with the *actus reus* at a later stage.

Authority:　*Kaitamaki* (1984). D was charged with rape. His defence was that when he penetrated the woman he thought she was consenting. When he realised that she objected he did not withdraw. The Privy Council held that the *actus reus* of rape was a continuing act, and when he realised that she did not consent (and he therefore formed the necessary *mens rea*) the *actus reus* was still in progress and there could therefore be coincidence.

One transaction

The second way the courts have dealt with the problem is to consider a continuing series of acts to be "one transaction" for the purposes of the criminal law. If *actus reus* and *mens rea* are both present at some time during this transaction, then there is liability.

Authority:　*Thabo Meli v R.* (1954). Ds had attempted to kill their victim by beating him over the head. Thinking him dead, they threw the body over a cliff. He died from the fall and exposure, and not from the beating. The Privy Council held that this was all one series of acts following through a preconceived plan of action and therefore could not be seen as separate acts at all. *Actus reus* and *mens rea* were present during some of the transaction, i.e. when they hit him over the head, and therefore Ds were guilty of murder.

Authority: *Church* (1966). The same reasoning was applied here even where there was no pre-conceived plan and D, mistakenly thinking he had killed the victim, disposed of the "body" in a canal thereby causing death. His manslaughter conviction was upheld on appeal.

Authority: *Le Brun* (1991). D committed an initial assault and then unintentionally killed what he believed to be a corpse in trying to cover up his crime. The Court of Appeal confirmed and applied the reasoning in *Church*.

This kind of reasoning is a way to avoid an unjust result.

Reforms

The Law Commission Report on Offences Against the Person and General Principles, No.218 (1994) is the most recent statement of recommended reforms in the area of *mens rea*.

Intention is defined as including knowledge that a result will occur in the ordinary course of events if D were to succeed in his purpose of causing some other result.

The report's definition of recklessness has effectively been incorporated into the law by the decision in *R. v G and another* (see p.17 above).

3. STRICT LIABILITY

There are some crimes for which, with regard to at least one element of the *actus reus*, (e.g. a particular circumstance or required consequence,) no *mens rea* is required. The defendant need not have intended or known about that circumstance or consequence. Liability is said to be strict with regard to that element.

It is untrue to say that crimes of strict liability never require *mens rea*. *Mens rea* may well be required with regard to other elements of the *actus reus*. It is only in extreme and rare cases where no *mens rea* is required for liability, thereby making the particular offence "absolute" (as apparently occurred in *Winzar v Chief Constable of Kent*—See Ch.1). Most strict liability crimes therefore are only "strict" as to one element of the *actus reus*.

1. PRESUMPTION OF REQUIREMENT FOR *MENS REA*

There is a presumption that *mens rea* is an essential ingredient in any offence.

Authority: *Sweet v Parsley* (1969). D was a landlady who did not live on the premises but visited only occasionally. Her lodgers smoked cannabis, though she was unaware of this. She was charged with being concerned in the management of premises which were used for the purposes of smoking cannabis contrary to s.5 of the (now repealed) Dangerous Drugs Act 1965. The magistrates and the Divisional Court held that no *mens rea* was necessary for this element of the *actus reus* and found her guilty. The House of Lords on further appeal quashed the conviction and said that this was not an offence of strict liability. Lord Reid re-stated the general principle that where a statute says nothing about *mens rea*, there is a presumption that *mens rea* will be required. If Parliament wished to create a crime of strict liability then it must make its intention manifest. In this case there would be no point in imposing strict liability since no degree of vigilance by the owner of the premises could prevent tenants smoking cannabis.

His Lordship also made the basic distinction between crimes which were truly criminal, where penalties were severe and *mens rea* should be required, and purely regulatory offences with minor penalties. These offences were "quasi-criminal" and strict liability was a practical and acceptable way of dealing with them. This explains one kind of strict liability offence but not the "protection of the public" type of offence. This explanation should be compared with the later one in *Gammon Ltd v Attorney-General* (see below).

Authority: *B v D.P.P.* (2000). A 15-year-old boy was charged with having incited a girl under the age of 14 to commit an act of gross indecency with him, contrary to s.1(1) of the Indecency with Children Act 1960. The House of Lords followed the approach laid down in *Sweet v Parsley* and, applying the usual presumption in favour of a requirement for *mens rea*, held that for a conviction under the section, the prosecution has to prove that the defendant was not mistaken. More precisely, the prosecution has to prove an absence of a genuine belief on the part of the accused, which does not have to be on reasonable grounds, that the victim was aged 14 or over. The presumption in favour of a requirement of *mens rea* is rebutted only if the need for a mental element is negatived by a compellingly clear implication. Such an implication may be found in the language used in the wording of the offence, the nature of the offence, the mischief sought to be prevented and any other circumstances which may assist in determining what intention is properly to be attributed to Parliament when creating the offence. [The decision in *B v D.P.P.* was followed and applied in *R. v K* (2001) where D was charged with indecent assault on a girl under 16 and the House of Lords held that D's mistaken belief (whether reasonable or not) that the girl was over 16 was a valid defence. *B v D.P.P.* and *R v K* have now been overtaken by the Sexual Offences Act 2003 which abolished a whole range of sexual offences, including those charged in these two cases, and enacted a new set of sexual offences. Now, in the case of a sexual offence against someone under 16, only a reasonable mistake that the victim is over 16 will be a defence—see pp.93–94 below.]

Broadly, there are two types of offence where the courts have found that the presumption in favour of a *mens rea* requirement has been rebutted and have thus been willing to impose strict liability. (See *Gammon (Hong Kong) Ltd v Attorney General*, below.)

Regulatory offences

One kind is the purely regulatory offence where no moral issue is at stake, the penalty is small, and from a practical point of view strict liability makes it easier to enforce these offences. Legislation relating to the sale of food provides a good example of this category. (See, e.g. *Smedleys Ltd v Breed*, p.26 below.)

Public danger offences

The second kind of offence is where the protection of the public is paramount. Here the penalty may be severe but strict liability is still felt necessary to induce the highest standard of care. The pollution cases are an example of this category, as are the dangerous drugs and weapons cases.

Authority: *Steele* (1993). D was charged under s.1(1)(a) of the Firearms Act 1968 with possession of a firearm without a certificate. He said he had been given a holdall containing a sawn-off shotgun minutes before police arrived, and that he did not know what was in it. The Court of Appeal confirmed his conviction and said it was irrelevant that he did not know, or even could not reasonably have known, what was in the bag. The legislation was obviously intended to be draconian.

2. SOME AREAS OF STRICT LIABILITY OFFENCES

There is no foolproof way of spotting in advance a strict liability crime, but there are certain kinds of offence and certain types of wording used in statutes, which are more likely to lead to the imposition of strict liability.

Dangerous drugs

There are several crimes concerning dangerous drugs where liability is strict. These offences fall into the category of protection of public safety.

Authority: *Marriott* (1971). D was in possession of a penknife which he knew had traces of a substance on it. This substance turned out to be a prohibited drug. The court held that D needed *mens rea* with regard to possession of a substance on the knife, but no *mens rea* with regard to the circumstance that the substance was a prohibited drug. It did not matter that he did not know, and could not reasonably have known, what the substance was.

However, this general policy in the dangerous drugs cases has its limits, see *Sweet v Parsley* (above).

Road traffic offences

Some road traffic offences where strict liability is imposed are of a regulatory, quasi-criminal nature while others are more serious.

Authority: *Bowsher* (1973). D was convicted of driving while disqualified even though he believed his disqualification had ended, and reasonably believed this, because his licence had been returned to him.

Another example is the offence of driving with an amount of alcohol in the bloodstream which is over the prescribed limit, contrary to s.5 of the Road Traffic Act 1988. *Mens rea* is not required with regard to the circumstance of having an amount of alcohol in the bloodstream over the prescribed limit.

Pollution

Crimes involving pollution often provide other examples of strict liability crimes designed to protect the public.

It is an offence under the Water Act 1989 to "cause" pollution of a river. Several cases have discussed the meaning of "cause" in this context.

Authority: *National Rivers Authority v Yorkshire Water Services* (1994). Y.W.S. operated a sewage works and one of its customers without its knowledge discharged forbidden effluent through Y.W.S.'s mechanisms. The Divisional Court held that "cause" does not imply either negligence or knowledge. Liability is therefore strict and Y.W.S. were liable.

Authority: *Attorney General's Reference No. 1 of 1994* (1995). Several D's had been involved at various stages in operating a sewage system and toxic sewage had polluted the river contrary to s.107 of the Water Act 1989, because of a failure properly to maintain the system. The Court of Appeal held that such failure could amount to "causing" within the wording of the Act despite its being an omission rather than an act. Whereas the alternative charge of "permitting" was qualified by the word "knowingly", there was no such limit on "causing", for which liability was strict.

Sale of food

This is another regulatory area which, given the number of cases and the work of the inspectorate, it is felt is best kept under control by strict liability.

   Authority: *Smedleys Ltd v Breed* (1974). D company was charged with selling food which was not of the substance demanded by the purchaser. A caterpillar had been found in a tin of peas from D company's factory. The House of Lords held D liable even though there were no other practicable preventive measures which could have been taken and the standard of care taken at the factory was extremely high.

   There are other areas where strict liability is prevalent, for example trade and industry, public health and liquor regulations.

3. DEFENCES

Some statutes imposing so-called strict liability now contain a limited form of defence, often based on lack of negligence. It can be argued that this trend is turning crimes of strict liability into crimes of negligence. Whether one considers this desirable depends on how strongly one is convinced of the arguments for and against strict liability (see below).

Sale of food

Under s.21 of the Food Safety Act 1990, D has a defence if he shows that he took all reasonable precautions and exercised all due diligence to avoid the commission of the offence by himself or a person under his control. This defence is commonly found in relation to statutory offences designed to protect consumers, e.g. in the Trade Descriptions Act 1968 and the Consumer Protection Act 1987. It is in effect a "no negligence" defence with the burden of proof on the defendant to show that he was not negligent.

Reverse burdens of proof

Sometimes a reverse burden of proof is incompatible with the European Convention on Human Rights, in which case the statutory provision is "read down" (i.e. interpreted) to impose on the defendant, not a legal burden but merely an evidential burden of proof. That was the result where the maximum penalty for the offence was life imprisonment and statute allowed the defendant a defence if he proved that he neither believed nor suspected nor had reason to suspect that the substance in his possession was a controlled drug: *Lambert* (2001). That was also the result where on a charge of professing to belong to a proscribed (terrorist) organisation, the statute provided that it was a defence for D to prove that he had not participated in the organisation's activities: *Att-Gen's Reference* (No.4 of 2002) (2004). On the other hand, where D was charged with driving when his blood alcohol level was above the prescribed limit, the House of Lords did not "read down" the legal burden on D to prove that there was no likelihood of his driving while in that condition: *Sheldrake* (2004).

4. REASONS FOR STRICT LIABILITY

The main reasons for imposing strict liability are:

(a) to protect the public from dangerous actions by creating a higher standard of care, and
(b) to regulate quasi-criminal activities in as efficient a manner as possible.

Authority: *Gammon (Hong Kong) Ltd v Attorney-General* (1984), in which the arguments in favour of strict liability are clearly set out. This was an example of a regulatory offence concerning breach of building regulations. The Privy Council held that, although there is a presumption of *mens rea* to be read into all offences, this can be displaced on clear evidence in two kinds of case:

(i) Cases of public protection where social danger exists.
(ii) Quasi-criminal offences of a regulatory nature.

The reasons for displacing the requirement of *mens rea* in such cases were said to be the encouraging of a higher standard of vigilance and ease of administration. Strict liability can also facilitate the control of corporate crime. Crimes committed by corporations are often under-reported and under-prosecuted, despite the consequences, both in terms of money and life, although in recent years prosecutions have been more common. Strict liability can help the control of corporate crime because it dispenses in some respects with the often difficult task of imputing the necessary *mens rea* to a sufficiently senior official within a corporation (see Ch.4).

5. REFORMS

The trend to modify strict liability is seen in the introduction of statutory defences. In Australia offences of strict liability have been mitigated by allowing a defence of all due care, a burden being on the defendant to prove his defence. This is one approach we have started to follow in this country and which could be more generally adopted—though it can raise human rights issues (see *Lambert* above).

This is not an area which attracts a lot of publicity or debate. Although many people think that there should be no strict liability and a minimum fault element of negligence should be required, others think the system works well in its present state and the administrative benefits outweigh any objections. Any major reform is unlikely.

4. PARTIES TO CRIME

It is not only the perpetrator who will be liable for a criminal offence. Other participants in the offence may also be liable. Under s.8 of the Accessories and Abettors Act 1861 as amended by the Criminal Law Act 1967:

> "Whosoever shall *aid, abet, counsel or procure* the commission of any indictable offence, whether the same be an offence at common law or by virtue of any Act passed or to be passed, shall be liable to be tried, indicted and punished as a principal offender."

Section 44 of the Magistrates' Courts Act 1980 makes a similar provision with respect to summary offences. Those involved in crimes to a lesser degree in this way are referred to as secondary parties and as a general rule their liability is the same as that of the principal. Where there is a discretion in sentencing, their degree of involvement will be taken into account.

The principal party must actually have committed the offence (or sometimes just the *actus reus* of it) before anyone can be liable as a secondary party. If that is not the case, there may be inchoate liability (see Ch.5).

1. PRINCIPALS

Joint principals

The principal is the main perpetrator of the offence: the one who commits the *actus reus* or the substantial part of the *actus reus*. It is possible to have more than one principal if more than one person is directly responsible for the *actus reus*. The test is whether someone contributes to the *actus reus* by his own independent act rather than merely aiding or abetting. See *Rogers*, pp.114–115 below.

Innocent agents

A principal may not always directly carry out the *actus reus* himself. He may use an innocent agent (e.g. *Cogan and Leak*, below).

2. SECONDARY PARTICIPATION

There are four kinds of secondary participation:

(i) Aiding,
(ii) Abetting,
(iii) Counselling
(iv) Procuring.

These four words have been held to have distinct meanings, although aiding and abetting are often charged together, as are counselling and procuring.

Authority: *Attorney General's Reference No. 1 of 1975.* The principal offender was driving with a blood-alcohol level over the prescribed limit. The secondary party had added alcohol to the principal's drink without his knowledge, knowing that he would be driving. Some general comments were made about secondary participation and the distinctions between the four modes of secondary participation.

Aiding

This is assisting the principal to commit the offence.

Abetting

This is providing encouragement. It implies that the principal derives (draws) some encouragement from the abettor.

Counselling

This involves giving advice. Counselling usually takes place prior to the commission of the crime and the counsellor may well not be present at the scene of the crime.

Authority: *Calhaem* (1985). D was charged with murder. She was said to have counselled Z to commit murder. Z gave evidence that despite D's instructions he had no intention of carrying out the killing. However, when he got to the victim's flat he had gone "berserk" and killed her. The jury was directed that counselling involved "putting somebody up to something" and that the acts carried out must be within the scope of the instructions. D was convicted and appealed on the basis that the jury should have been directed that there had to be a causal connection between the counselling and the act, and here there was not. The court held that there was no requirement of a causal connection in counselling, and the conviction was affirmed.

Procuring

This means to "produce by endeavour". It is unnecessary for the principal to know about the procuring, but procuring does imply a causal connection. *The Attorney General's Reference No. 1 of 1975* case (above) was an example where the procuring was without the knowledge and consent of the principal but was the cause of the offence.

3. ASSISTANCE AFTER THE COMMISSION OF AN ARREST-ABLE OFFENCE

Assistance given after the commission of the offence, to enable someone to escape or dispose of evidence or proceeds for example, does not come within the definitions of aiding, abetting, counselling or procuring. It is a separate offence intentionally to impede the apprehension or prosecution of an arrestable offender (s.4 of the Criminal Law Act 1967).

4. PRESENCE AT THE SCENE OF THE CRIME

Merely witnessing an offence and omitting to try to stop or report it does not amount to secondary participation.

Authority: *Wilcox v Jeffrey* (1951). D was present at a concert given by someone who was performing in the country in contravention of the Aliens Order 1920. He had met the performer at the airport beforehand and later praised the performance in a magazine. The court held that this was sufficient evidence of encouragement to constitute secondary participation.

Authority: *Jefferson* (1994). D and others were present during widespread public disorder after a televised football game. There was no evidence of their violence but the prosecution claimed that their presence had actively encouraged others to violence. They were correctly convicted as secondary participants under ss.1 and 2 of the Public Order Act 1986, and appealed. The court held that where the presence of D encouraged and was intended to encourage violence, aiding and abetting was established.

5. PARTICIPATION BY OMISSION

Failing to prevent an offence can amount to participating in it where a person is in a position to prevent it because he is in control of property or for some other reason.

Authority: *Tuck v Robinson* (1970). D was the licensee of a public house. He allowed his customer to drink after hours and thereby commit offences. His inactivity was held to constitute aiding and abetting because he was in a position of authority and control and therefore under a duty to act.

Authority: *Bland* (1987). D lived with someone who was guilty of possession of drugs. Her conviction for aiding and abetting him was quashed on appeal. The court found that there was no evidence of active or passive assistance. Living in the same room was not enough.

6. *MENS REA* OF SECONDARY PARTIES

Knowledge

Secondary participants need both *mens rea* as to their own *actus reus* and knowledge of, or at least wilful blindness as to, the circumstances of the offence. This is so even in relation to strict liability offences.

Authority: *Callow v Tillstone* (1900). D was a veterinary surgeon who had examined a carcass and negligently certified it as sound. The principal was strictly liable for selling unfit food, but D's conviction as a secondary participant was quashed because he had been merely negligent and had not *known* that the meat was unsound.

Authority: *Webster* (2006). D, who owned a car, allowed one of his passengers, W, whom he knew to have been drinking, to take over the driving. W drove erratically at excessive speed with the result that another of the passengers was thrown out of the car and killed. D was charged with aiding and abetting W to cause death by dangerous driving. The Court of Appeal held that D could not be convicted unless the jury was satisfied that, when he allowed W to take over, D had foreseen the possibility that W would drive dangerously. Alternatively if the prosecution based its case on D's failure to intervene after W had begun to drive, it would have to be shown that D had known that W was driving dangerously at a time when there was an opportunity to intervene.

The secondary party need not know all the details of the offence to be committed but he must have an idea of the type of offence or have a series of possible offences in mind.

Authority: *Bainbridge* (1960). D had purchased some oxygen cutting equipment on behalf of a third party who he knew was going to use it for an illegal purpose, although he was not sure what that purpose was. The court held that D, to be liable, would need to know more than that the purpose was illegal. Although he did not need to know all the details he would need to know, for example, that it was going to be used for breaking and entering.

Authority: *D.P.P. for Northern Ireland v Maxwell* (1978). D was a member of a terrorist organisation. He was told to drive some men to a cinema. He knew that their purpose was illegal but he did not know the specific details. In fact they planted a bomb. He was convicted of abetting an act done with intent to cause an unlawful explosion. The House of Lords held that he did not need to know the precise weapon and method to be used by the others. He knew they were terrorists. He knew their purpose would be to endanger life or property. That was enough.

This is even more general than *Bainbridge*, and widens the scope of liability.

Where the offence is *procuring* the commission of a crime, recklessness as to whether the principal will commit the crime, is not sufficient *mens rea* for the secondary party.

Authority: *Blakely, Sutton* (1991). Ds had spiked their victim's drink intending to tell him before he left to drive home so that he would then have to walk home. In fact he left before they had a chance to tell him. He was stopped by police and convicted of driving with an excess of alcohol in the bloodstream. Ds contended that they had never intended that he commit such an offence and they had not realised that he might leave before they could tell him what they had done. On appeal their convictions were quashed. Although not necessary for the decision, their Lordships expressed the opinion that only intention would suffice.

Joint enterprise

In a joint criminal enterprise, two requirements must be satisfied before D can be liable as a secondary party for an act of the principal offender.

1. The principal's act must be within the scope of the joint enterprise. This means that it must be an act contemplated by D, i.e. not fundamentally different from any kind of act foreseen by D. D has no criminal liability at all in respect of the principal's acts which are outside the scope of the joint enterprise, e.g. where D foresees only the use of fists to beat up the intended victim and the principal attacks the victim using a lethal weapon which D did not even know the principal had.

2. D must have foreseen that the principal would commit the *actus reus* of the full offence and that the principal would do so with the requisite *mens rea* for the full offence.

Authority: *Powell, English* (1997). P and D and one other man visited a drug dealer. One of them, possibly the third man, killed the drug dealer. P and D were convicted (as secondary parties) of murder. In a different case, E took part with W in a joint enterprise to attack a police officer and to injure him with wooden posts. In the course of the attack, W used a knife with which he stabbed the policeman to death. E was convicted (as secondary party) of murder. The House of Lords heard both appeals together. Their Lordships upheld P's and D's convictions but quashed that of E. They held: (1) it is sufficient to found a conviction for murder for a secondary party to have realised that in the course of the joint enterprise, the principal might kill with intent to do so or with intent to cause grievous bodily harm; (2) where, however, the principal offender kills with a deadly weapon which the secondary party did not know that he had and therefore did not foresee the use of, the secondary party is not guilty of murder. However,

> ". . . if the weapon used by the primary party is different to, but as dangerous as, the weapon which the secondary party contemplated he might use, the secondary party should not escape liability for murder because of the difference in the weapon, for example, if he foresaw that the primary party might use a gun to kill and the latter used a knife to kill, or *vice versa*."

Even though the principal offender can be liable for murder only if he intended death or grievous bodily harm, the secondary offender does not have to have had such an intention. Nor does he have to have "authorised" or "agreed to" the principal's actions. It is sufficient that he took part in the enterprise, with foresight that the principal might kill with the requisite *mens rea*, i.e. intention. The same is true in the case of attempted crime, where the principal offender can be guilty only if he intended to commit the full offence but another person can be convicted provided he participated in the enterprise with foresight that the principal offender might intentionally attempt the full offence: *O'Brien* (1995).

Where the secondary party, e.g. in a joint enterprise situation, is not a party to the act of the principal offender (e.g. where the principal offender uses a weapon which the secondary party did not even know he had), then the secondary party is not liable at all in respect of that act of the principal offender. Apart from that situation, it is possible for the secondary party to be guilty of the same offence as the principal offender or of a greater or lesser offence—depending on the *mens rea* of the secondary party: *Gilmour* (2000). Thus in homicide, where the secondary party is party to the principal's act, but does not foresee that the principal offender might kill with intent to do so or with intent to cause grievous bodily harm, then the secondary party could be guilty of the lesser offence of manslaughter, i.e. provided the secondary party foresaw that the principal offender might inflict actual bodily harm.

Authority: *Stewart and Schofield* (1995). Ds went with a third party to carry out a robbery, taking a pole. The third party beat the victim to death with the pole and was convicted of murder. The Ds were convicted of manslaughter. They appealed claiming that they should have been convicted of murder or nothing. Dismissing their appeal, the Court of Appeal held that in a joint enterprise case where the secondary party was party to the fatal act but only had *mens rea* appropriate for a lesser offence, he would be liable for that lesser offence.

For the possibility of a secondary party being liable for a *more* serious offence than the principal offender, see *Howe* p.37 below.

7. ACQUITTAL OF PRINCIPAL OFFENDER

If there is no principal offender this does not necessarily present a problem. Providing it can be proved that an offence or, at least, the *actus reus* of an offence was committed, a secondary participant can be convicted.

The situation can be complicated if a principal offender is acquitted. Such an acquittal does not necessarily mean that no offence has been committed and therefore the above reasoning can be applied and secondary participants convicted.

No *actus reus* of an offence

If the acquittal of a principal offender means that no *actus reus* of an offence has been committed, then there can be no secondary liability.

Authority: *Thornton v Mitchell* (1940). A conductor of a bus was charged as a secondary party to careless driving after helping a driver to reverse. The driver was acquitted on the basis of no carelessness. The conductor was acquitted too. If there was no careless driving, there could be no aiding and abetting of it.

Acquittal for other reasons

If there is an *actus reus* then there can still be secondary liability (for procuring the offence) even if the alleged principal offender is not guilty for some other reason, e.g. no *mens rea* or a valid defence.

Authority: *Cogan and Leak* (1976). D had persuaded a friend to have intercourse with his (D's) wife. The friend had honestly but unreasonably believed the wife was consenting and was therefore (on the law as it then was) not guilty of rape. However, the *actus reus* of rape had been committed. Thus it was possible for a secondary party who had not believed in the wife's consent to be liable. Such was D but he was also her husband and a husband at that time could not be guilty of raping his wife. The court nevertheless upheld his conviction on two alternative bases; (i) he was liable as secondary party for procuring the commission of the *actus reus* by his friend; (ii) he was liable as principal offender acting through the innocent agency of his friend. [Note that a husband can now be guilty as principal offender of rape of his wife: *R*. (1992),]

Authority: *Millward* (1994). D, knowing that his vehicle was defective, instructed B, his employee to drive it. A fatal accident occurred because of the defect. B was acquitted of causing death by reckless driving but D was convicted. On appeal, D's conviction was upheld on the basis that he had procured the commission of the *actus reus* of the offence. A procurer can be guilty even though the principal is not guilty because of lack of *mens rea*.

Authority: *Wheelhouse* (1994). W provided P with a key to a garage at a house, a key to a car inside the garage and a map showing how to get to the house. P believed the car to belong to W. P entered the garage and removed the car. W and P were charged with burglary. P was acquitted but W's conviction was upheld on the basis that he had had dishonest intent and had procured the commission of the *actus reus* by P.

Cogan and Leak, Millward and *Wheelhouse* were all decisions reached on the basis that the secondary party can be convicted of "procuring" the *actus reus*, even though the principal is not guilty because of lack of mens rea. It is not clear whether someone can be convicted of "aiding", "abetting" or "counselling" where the principal lacks the *mens rea* for the offence. In *R. v Powell, R. v English* (above) the House of Lords held that a secondary party can be guilty if he foresaw that the primary party would commit the *actus reus* with the requisite *mens rea*. This seems to suggest that normally for a secondary offender to be liable, the primary offender must not only commit the *actus reus* but must do so with the requisite *mens rea*. If that is so, then the situation where someone can be convicted of "procuring" an offence by a primary party who lacks *mens rea*, is an exception. Exception or not, it is well established, fortified by the decision of the House of Lords in *Howe* (1987), that a secondary party can be guilty of "procuring" an offence, even though that may be a more serious offence than that of which the principal offender is guilty—or even if the principal offender has a complete defence and is not guilty of any offence at all. This could occur, for example, where the principal offender has some defence, such as duress, which is specific to himself.

8. REPENTANCE OF SECONDARY PARTY

If an alleged secondary party repents before the offence is committed then he may escape liability if he withdraws at a sufficiently early stage, communicates that withdrawal une-quivocally to the other participant(s) and does all he reasonably can to avert commission of the crime.

Authority: *Baker* (1994). D had initially taken part in a knife attack, then stopped, turned away and said he no longer wanted to carry out the attack. The court held that this was not enough to avoid liability. D had to dissociate himself completely from the crime occurring at all, and not just from his part in it. What constitutes effective withdrawal depends on the facts of each case and is for the jury to decide.

An unequivocal communication to the other parties is not necessary in the case of spontaneous (as opposed to pre-planned) violence. In that case simply walking away is sufficient, though it will not absolve D from criminal liability for earlier acts committed while he was still a party to the violence: *Mitchell* (1998). Where death has resulted and D is charged with being a party to murder, D is not guilty unless it is established that the fatal injuries were inflicted while D was still acting within the joint enterprise.

Authority: *O'Flaherty, Ryan and Toussant* (2004). A street fight occurred between two groups of men. One group included O, R, T and others. O, R and T used weapons: a cricket bat, a hammer, a beer bottle. When the fight moved to a nearby street, R and T did not follow. The deceased, H, a member of the other group, died of injuries received. In the second street, O, still holding the cricket bat, was seen to move within a few feet of H's prone body, though he was not seen to use the bat at this stage. There was no evidence that any injury causative of death was inflicted in the first street. R and T's convictions were quashed because a person who disengages from the joint enterprise before the commission of the crime is not liable for that crime. O's conviction was upheld. He was present and at least providing encouragement.

9. VICTIMS AS SECONDARY PARTIES

Sometimes a statutory offence is created specifically for the protection of a particular category of persons, e.g. minors. Someone in that category who is victim of the offence cannot be liable as a secondary party.

Authority: *Tyrrell* (1894). D, a girl between 13 and 16, encouraged X to have unlawful sexual intercourse with her. It was held that she was not guilty of aiding and abetting him since she was in the category of persons the offence was created to protect.

10. CORPORATE LIABILITY

Corporations, such as limited companies, are legal entities, but there are obvious problems regarding their participation in a criminal offence as regards *mens rea*. Although they cannot, practically speaking, form any necessary *mens rea*, criminal liability is imposed upon corporations in two ways:

(a) Vicarious liability

A corporation is vicariously liable for the acts of its employees or agents in normal situations of vicarious liability (see below).

(b) The identification principle

Certain key individuals are the company's mind and will. They are identified with the company. Thus if one or more of them, in the course of the company's business, commits a crime (with the necessary *mens rea*), then the company is guilty of the offence; their *mens rea is* the *mens rea* of the company. Normally, only the directors (and perhaps the company secretary) are sufficiently senior to be regarded as part of the company's mind and will; the *mens rea* of a mere store manager of a Tesco supermarket is not to be attributed to the company: *Tesco v Nattrass* (1972).

An exception occurs in certain statutory offences whereby the proper construction of the statute may indicate that the mind of some other person (other, and less senior, than a director) is to be used for the attribution of knowledge or *mens rea* to the company: *Meridian Global Fund Management Ltd v Securities Commission* (1995). That person may, as in *Meridian*, be the company employee who handled the particular transaction in question. Similarly, under the Health and Safety at Work Act 1974, it is an employer's duty to ensure, so far as reasonably practicable, the health and safety of employees and non-employees. The proper construction of that Act means that the company/employer will be guilty unless all reasonable precautions were taken, not just by the directors at board level, but by its other relevant servants or agents: *Gateway Foods* (1997).

Authority: *Tesco v London Borough of Brent* (1993). The company was charged, under the Video Recordings Act 1984, with selling a video film with an "18" classification to a 14–year-old. The company relied (unsuccessfully) on a statutory defence that it "neither knew nor had reasonable grounds to believe" the buyer to be under 18. It was held that, on a proper construction of the Act, the knowledge of the sales assistant who sold the video was to be attributed to the company.

The rule in *Tesco v Nattrass* used to mean that a prosecution of a company for manslaughter by gross negligence had to fail unless there was proof of the guilt (of the same crime) of a human being (normally a director) with whom the company could be identified: *Att-Gen.'s Reference No.2 of 1999*. That position was rectified by Corporate Manslaughter and Corporate Homicide Act 2007 which created a specific offence of corporate manslaughter requiring proof of management failings at a senior level but not necessarily at board level (see p.118 below).

11. VICARIOUS LIABILITY

Vicarious liability does not exist as a general principle, as it does in the law of tort. There are, however, three types of situation where vicarious criminal liability can arise under statute.

(a) Express vicarious liability

For example s.165 of the Licensing Act 1964 provides:

> "If any person in licensed premises himself *or by his servant or agent* sells or supplies to any person as the measure of intoxicating liquor for which he asks an amount exceeding that measure, he shall be liable to a fine. . .".

(b) Delegated management

Where an employer is under a statutory duty, and delegates his managerial and proprietary functions duty to an employee, he will be vicariously liable for any criminal offence—even one requiring *mens rea*—which the employee "commits" while carrying out that duty.

(c) Vicarious liability implied by statute

No delegation is required for this type of vicarious liability to be imposed. It occurs where the statutory wording is equally applicable to both employer and employee—where the *actus reus* is, for example, to "sell", to "be in possession of", to "keep", to "use". Usually such offences are crimes of strict liability.

Authority: *National Rivers Authority v Alfred McAlpine Homes (East) Ltd* (1994). The company was charged with "causing polluted matter, wet cement, to enter" a stream, contrary to the Water Resources Act 1991, s.85. The Divisional Court held that the company was criminally liable for "causing" pollution which resulted from the acts or omissions of its employees acting within the course and scope of their employment, irrespective of whether they were the controlling mind and will of the company.

12. REFORMS

In its Report No. 305 *Participating in Crime* (2007), The Law Commission recommended replacing the common law rules on secondary liability and innocent agency with a statutory scheme of offences. The new offences would catch someone who "assists" or "encourages". "Counselling" and "procuring" would drop out of the terminology of secondary offences.

Proposed statutory secondary offences

These offences would apply where P commits the conduct element (the *actus reus*) of the principal offence. They state when D would be liable as secondary party to that offence.

Secondary liability: offence 1:

D assists or encourages P to commit the conduct element of the principal offence, intending P to commit it.

Secondary liability: offence 2:

D is party to a joint criminal venture with P and P commits a crime within the scope of the joint criminal venture. The existence or scope of a joint criminal venture may be inferred from the conduct of the participants (whether or not there is an express agreement).

Proposed innocent agency offence

D would be liable as a principal offender if he intentionally caused an innocent agent, P, to commit the conduct element of the principal offence. P would be an innocent agent if the only reason that he was not himself guilty of the offence was that he was under 10, had a defence of insanity or acted without the fault element (the *mens rea*) for the offence.

Proposed offence of causing a no-fault offence

This proposed offence would catch the person who causes another to commit an offence of strict liability, e.g. causing someone to "drink/drive" by spiking his drinks.

Defences

The proposals would

(a) retain the defence (as in *Tyrell*) for a victim who is in a class of persons whom an offence was intended to protect, and

(b) provide a defence for someone acting reasonably to prevent the commission of an offence or the occurrence of harm (e.g. diverting P's intention to injure someone into an intention instead to damage property).

Inchoate secondary offences

For two proposed new inchoate secondary offences applicable where the principal offender does not commit the principal offence, see p.53 below.

---

5. INCHOATE OFFENCES

Incitement, conspiracy and attempt cover the preparatory stages of other criminal offences. They are substantive offences in themselves and, unlike liability for secondary participation in a crime, it is unnecessary that the main offence be committed. Indeed it is often unlikely, and in some cases impossible, that it will be.

1. INCITEMENT

An inciter is someone who tries to help, influence, encourage, threaten or pressurise another party to commit a crime. The crime incited may or may not actually be committed; it is irrelevant to the liability of the inciter, except that he may become a secondary participant if it is committed.

Mens rea in incitement

Incitement is a crime of specific intent. The *mens rea* required is that the inciter intends the person incited to commit an act which, if done, would be a criminal offence. It is irrelevant whether the inciter (or the person incited) believes it to be a criminal offence.

Inciting the impossible

This is governed by the common law and not by statute. There can be liability for incitement only if the commission of the crime incited was possible at the time of the incitement.

Authority: *Fitzmaurice* (1983). D's father had asked D to recruit someone to rob a woman on her way with wages to a bank. Believing the robbery was to take place, D recruited B and encouraged him to take part in the proposed robbery. In fact the proposed robbery was not really intended to occur but was part of D's father's plan to enable him to collect reward money for informing on a (in fact false) robbery. D was convicted of incitement to rob. On appeal it was held that (1) it is no offence to incite someone to commit an offence which at the time of the incitement is impossible of commission (e.g. inciting a non pregnant woman to have an unlawful abortion); (2) in this case the robbery, though unlikely to occur, was not an impossibility at the time of D's incitement of B. (Note: the law on inciting the impossible is different from the law on conspiring to commit or attempting to commit the impossible. Parliament has legislated to make it an offence to conspire to commit, or to attempt, the impossible. Incitement on the other hand is still subject to the common law.)

It is not the crime of incitement to incite some to commit an act which is not criminal: *Whitehouse* (1977).

Authority: *Claydon* (2005). D was convicted of inciting a boy of 13 to commit buggery. At the time, a boy under 14 was in law conclusively presumed to be incapable of sexual intercourse. The Court of Appeal quashed D's conviction applying the rule in *Whitehouse*. Since it would not be criminal for the boy to commit buggery, it was not a crime to incite him to do it. In obiter dicta, the Court stated that in the crime of incitement the intention or knowledge of the person incited is irrelevant. *Curr* (1968) which had stated otherwise was wrongly decided. The focus of incitement is on the acts and intentions of the inciter.

2. CONSPIRACY

A conspiracy is an agreement by two or more persons: (i) to commit a crime; (ii) to defraud someone, or; (iii) to corrupt public morals or outrage public decency. The limits of conspiracy are controlled by the Criminal Law Act 1977, which left the latter two categories intact only as a temporary measure, as major reforms in those areas were being considered. Conspiracy is therefore governed partly by the common law and partly by statute.

Statutory conspiracy

Conspiracies to commit criminal offences fall under s.1(1) of the Criminal Law Act 1977 which provides:

"Subject to the following provisions of this Part of this Act, if a person agrees with any other person or persons that a course of conduct shall be pursued which, if the agreement is carried out in accordance with their intentions, either—

(a) will necessarily amount to or involve the commission of any offence or offences by one or more of the parties to the agreement, or—
(b) would do so but for the existence of facts which render the commission of the offence or any of the offences impossible,

he is guilty of conspiracy to commit the offence or offences in question."

Under s.1(2):

"Where liability for any offence may be incurred without knowledge on the part of the person committing it of any particular fact or circumstance necessary for the commission of the offence, a person shall nevertheless not be guilty of conspiracy to commit that offence by virtue of subsection (1) above unless he and at least one other party to the agreement intend or know that that fact or circumstance shall or will exist at the time when the conduct constituting the offence is to take place."

These subsections make it clear that the mens rea for conspiracy is intention only and not recklessness. Knowledge or intention is required as to circumstances, not merely suspicion, even with respect to crimes of strict liability.

Authority: *Saik* (2006). D was charged with conspiracy (contrary to s.1(1) of the Criminal Law Act 1977) to commit the offence of money laundering by converting bank notes. The substantive offence of money laundering (in s.93C(2) of the Criminal Justice Act 1988) required proof that the defendant knew or had reasonable grounds to suspect that the property represented the proceeds of crime. D pleaded guilty to the conspiracy charge subject to the qualification that he did not "know" but only "suspected" that the money was the proceeds of crime. The House of Lords quashed his conviction. Although suspicion that the money was the proceeds of crime would be sufficient on a charge of the substantive offence, knowledge of that fact was required for a conviction of conspiracy to commit that offence. Whenever the existence of a particular fact or circumstance is required for the commission of the substantive offence, s.1(2) requires that, to be guilty of conspiracy, the defendant must intend or know that fact or circumstance shall or will exist when the conspiracy is to be carried into effect.

Authority: *Anderson* (1986). D had agreed to supply wire-cutters to be used in a gaol break, but claimed that he never intended the plan to go ahead, and did not believe it would succeed. The House of Lords held *ratio decidendi* that it was not necessary for liability that he intended the plan to go ahead. Therefore there could apparently be a conspiracy even when none of the conspirators ever intends the plan to be put into action. The House of Lords held obiter dicta that a defendant would only be guilty of conspiracy if he planned to play some active part in the carrying out of the agreement. Both aspects of the decision in *Anderson* were unfortunate. The *ratio decidendi* has been ignored in later cases, including *Edwards* (1991) where the defendant had agreed to supply amphetamine and the Court of Appeal held that the trial judge had been correct in directing the jury not to convict the defendant of conspiring to supply amphetamine unless they were sure that he intended to supply it. In *Siracusa* (1986) the Court of Appeal "explained" the obiter dicta in *Anderson*, saying that there can be active or passive participation and that an intention to participate in furtherance of the crime can be shown by a failure to stop the criminal acts of other conspirators.

Although there must be more than one person to form a conspiracy, it is only necessary that one of the co-conspirators be capable of carrying out the offence.

Authority: *Sherry* (1993). Two Ds were indicted for a conspiracy to abduct a son of one of them, contrary to the Child Abduction Act 1984, s.1. Only one of them was a specified person capable of committing the s.1 offence, but that was sufficient for the purposes of their conspiracy liability.

Conspiracy at common law

The only conspiracies left at common law are conspiracy to defraud, conspiracy to corrupt public morals and conspiracy to outrage public decency, although outraging public decency may well be a criminal offence in itself and therefore covered by s.1.

Conspiracy to defraud

There are two alternative types of conspiracy to defraud, each requiring proof of a plan to use deceit or other dishonest means. One is a conspiracy to "cause the victim economic loss by depriving him of some property or right . . . to which he is or would or might become entitled." The other is a conspiracy to cause a person performing public duties to act contrary to his public duty.

Authority: *Scott v Metropolitan Police Commissioner* (1975). D and others agreed to copy certain films without permission and without paying fees, and to make money by showing these copies and charging for admission. There was no deception involved and therefore an offence under the Theft Act 1968 was difficult to prove. The House of Lords held that this was a conspiracy to defraud and deceit was unnecessary for that offence if the plan involved the use of other dishonest means.

A conspiracy need not be such that, if carried out, it would definitely cause an individual to suffer loss. It is sufficient if it would put his economic or proprietary interests at risk: *Allsop* (1976).

Authority: *Wai Yu Tsang* (1992). D had agreed with others dishonestly not to enter certain dishonoured cheques on the records of the bank, in order to save the bank's reputation. The Privy Council held that the motive was irrelevant as was the fact that no loss was actually caused. It was sufficient that the plan involved imperilling the economic interests of others.

Authority: *Hollinshead* (1985). Ds manufactured and marketed devices the only purpose of which was, when fitted to an electricity meter, to falsify the record of electricity consumed. They were guilty of conspiracy to defraud the electricity companies even though the defrauding would be done, not by them, but by third parties (those who eventually bought the devices). This is a different rule from that which applies in statutory conspiracies—see Criminal Law Act 1977, s.1(1) above.

If a fact situation amounts to both a conspiracy to commit a crime and a conspiracy to defraud, the prosecution is free to charge either offence: Criminal Law Act 1977, s.5 as amended by Criminal Justice Act 1988, s.12.

Conspiracy to corrupt public morals

This offence first appeared in a modern case in 1963.

Authority: *Shaw v Director of Public Prosecutions* (1963). D published a "Ladies Directory" containing details of prostitutes and was charged with conspiring with the prostitutes to corrupt public morals. The House of Lords held that there was such an offence at common law, and affirmed D's conviction.

Later cases restricted the application of the case.

Authority: *D.P.P. v Withers* (1975). D and others had by deceit induced people to part with information which it was against their duty to disclose. The House of Lords rejected the suggestion that *Shaw* had created an offence of conspiracy to effect a public mischief and held that no such offence existed.

Authority: *Knuller v D.P.P.* (1973). D and others published advertisements in a contact magazine aimed at male homosexuals. The House of Lords held that this was a conspiracy to corrupt public morals, thus confirming that this offence did exist. However, their Lordships explained that the jury needed to be directed to consider whether the people likely to read the material were likely to be depraved and corrupted and "deprave and corrupt" were strong words meaning more than just leading morally astray. Their Lordships also firmly rejected the idea put forward in *Shaw* that the House had a residual power to create new common law offences.

Conspiracy to outrage public decency

Outraging public decency is itself an offence. Thus a conspiracy to commit it is now a statutory conspiracy under s.1.

Authority: *Gibson* (1990). The defendant, an artist, had included in a public display of his work a pair of earrings made from freeze dried foetuses. He was convicted of the common law offence of outraging public decency.

Authority: *Knuller v D.P.P.* (See above). The concept of outraging public decency was defined in very strong terms, and was said to go ". . . considerably beyond offending the susceptibilities of, or even shocking, reasonable people."

Conspiracy to do the impossible

Since the Criminal Law Act 1977 was amended by the Criminal Attempts Act 1981, the law relating to impossible conspiracies is now in line with that relating to impossible attempts. It follows that, for example, where two people agree to extract cocaine from a substance in their possession which, unknown to them, contains no cocaine, they will, despite the impossibility of achieving their objective, nevertheless be guilty of conspiring to produce a controlled drug. The leading authority on impossible attempts, *Shivpuri* (see below), can therefore be applied by analogy to impossible conspiracies. For a discussion of the different types of impossibility see below, under Impossible Attempts.

3. ATTEMPTS

The law relating to liability for attempts is now governed by the Criminal Attempts Act 1981. Under s.(1) of the Act:

> "If, with intent to commit an offence to which this section applies, a person does an act which is more than merely preparatory to the commission of the offence, he is guilty of attempting to commit the offence."

Section 1 applies to (and thus it is a crime to attempt) indictable offences and offences triable either way. The latter includes offences (such as theft) which can be tried either summarily or on indictment. It is not a crime to attempt to commit a summary offence.

Proximity

The question of whether an act is more than merely preparatory is a question of fact to be left to the jury. The judge must not usurp the jury's functions. The common law tests of proximity, such as the "last act" test and the "equivocality" test, have been superseded by the test in the Act.

   Authority: *Gullefer* (1986). D tried to distract dogs in a greyhound race in order to get a call of "no race" and so retrieve his stake. He was charged with attempted theft. The case turned on whether what he had done was "more than merely preparatory" to the commission of the theft. At trial the "Rubicon test"—has the defendant "burnt his boats" and reached the point of no return—was referred to. On appeal this test was rejected. The specific pre-1981 tests do not apply. It is a question of fact for the jury, based on the wording of the Act.
   Usually activities such as getting equipped, reconnoitring the scene, lying in the wait, etc., will not amount to more than preparation. There is, however, no rule of thumb for distinguishing between mere preparation and an attempt.

   Authority: *Geddes* (1996). D had entered the grounds of a school and was found in the boys' toilet by a member of staff.

He ran away discarding a rucksack containing lengths of string, sealing tape and other items. He was convicted of attempting to imprison a person unknown and appealed. The Court of Appeal held that, although he undoubtedly had the necessary intention, the evidence showed no more than that he had made preparations, got himself ready and put himself in a position to commit the offence of imprisonment. He had not moved from the role of preparation into that of execution or implementation.

Authority: *Tosti* (1997). Ds had oxyacetylene equipment, drove to the scene of a planned burglary, concealed the equipment in a hedge, approached the door of a barn and examined the padlock on it. At that point they realised they were being watched and ran off. They appealed against their convictions for attempted burglary. It was held, dismissing their appeal, that there was evidence that they had done an act which showed that they had actually attempted to commit the offence. The judge had been correct to leave the issue to the jury.

Mens rea for attempts

The *mens rea* of an attempt is set out in s.1(1) of the Act: "If *with intent* to commit an offence . . .". Attempt is a crime of specific intent and only intent will suffice. The Criminal Law Act has made no change in this respect. This requirement does not however apply to the *mens rea* for the circumstances of an offence.

Authority: *Khan* (1990). D was charged with attempted rape. He had attempted to have intercourse with a woman, being reckless as to whether or not she consented. He was found guilty and appealed on the basis that in order to be liable for attempt it should be proved that he knew (or intended) that she did not consent. Dismissing his appeal, the Court of Appeal held that s.1(1) of the 1981 Act required intent only as to the act and any consequence. The requisite *mens rea* for the circumstances relevant to the offence was the same as for the complete offence: in this case recklessness. [The *mens rea* required for the full offence of rape has since been changed, see Sexual Offences Act 2003, s.1(1) at p.91 below.]

Authority: *Attorney General's Reference No.3 of 1992* (1994). Ds were charged with attempted aggravated arson, i.e. attempting to damage property and being reckless as to whether the life of another would be endangered thereby. They threw a petrol bomb from a moving car at a stationary car and the bomb hit a pavement and a wall. There was no evidence that they intended to endanger life. The Court of Appeal held that recklessness as to the circumstances of endangering life was sufficient for attempt liability, provided they intended to cause the criminal damage.

The situation with regard to consequences is more straightforward.

Authority: *Mohan* (1976). D refused to stop his car when signalled by a P.C. Instead he drove straight at the P.C. who managed to avoid him. He was convicted of attempting to cause grievous bodily harm. His conviction was quashed because the jury had been misdirected regarding *mens rea* for attempt. The Court of Appeal defined the necessary *mens rea* as intention, i.e.:

> "a decision to bring about, insofar as it lies within the accused's power, the commission of the offence which it is alleged the accused attempted to commit, no matter whether the accused desired that consequence or no."

This excludes recklessness and foresight of probable or likely consequences. It is the same as the concept of intention put forward in *Nedrick, Woollin*, etc. This is still the case after the 1981 Act.

Authority: *Walker and Hayles* (1990). Ds had thrown their victim off a third floor balcony and seriously injured him. They were convicted of attempted murder and appealed on the basis that the meaning of intention in attempts was restricted to purpose or direct intent. The Court of Appeal, affirming their convictions, made it clear that intention has only one meaning. The cases on homicide are applicable to all cases of intent.

Attempting the impossible

Under s.1(2) of the Act:

> "A person may be guilty of attempting to commit an offence to which this section applies even though the facts are such that the commission of the offence is impossible."

Section 1(3) states:

"In any case where—
(a) apart from this subsection a person's intention would not be regarded as having amounted to an intent to commit an offence; but
(b) if the facts of the case had been as he believed them to be, his intention would be so regarded, then for the purposes of subsection (1) above he shall be regarded as having an intent to commit that offence."

However the first case to go to the House of Lords gave an unlikely interpretation of the Act.

Authority: *Anderton v Ryan* (1985). D was charged with attempting to dishonestly handle a video recorder. D had received it believing it to be stolen but the police could not produce positive evidence that it was stolen and the case had to proceed on the basis that it was not. The House of Lords held that no section of the Act made it an offence to attempt to do something which if the defendant had done all he intended to do, would not have been a crime. That was the case here.

Shivpuri has now overruled *Anderton v Ryan* and reinterpreted the Act. Lord Bridge, who gave one of the leading judgements in *Anderton v Ryan* also gave judgment in *Shivpuri* and the issues were reassessed.

Authority: *Shivpuri* (1986). D was convicted of attempting to be knowingly concerned in dealing with a prohibited drug. He brought through customs what he thought was a prohibited drug but was in fact a harmless substance. The House of Lords held that on the true construction of s.1 of the Criminal Attempts Act 1981 D was guilty, even if the facts were such that the actual offence was impossible of commission. All that was needed was an act more than merely preparatory to the commission of the offence D *intended* to commit. Such an act was present in this case. There was no clear distinguishing principle to differentiate *Anderton v Ryan*. It was clear from the Law Commission's Report on Attempt and Impossibility that the *Anderton v Ryan* fact situation was intended to be covered by the Act. *Anderton v Ryan* was therefore overruled.

Shivpuri thus confirms that attempting the impossible can be a crime. A defendant will be guilty of an attempt to commit a crime if he does an act which is more than merely preparatory towards that crime, even if the commission of the full offence is either factually or legally impossible for any reason. Trying to pick an empty pocket is a good example. It amounts to attempted theft.

Authority: *Jones* (2007). D sent a series of explicit text messages to someone he believed was a girl aged 12 but was in fact a grown woman. In them he arranged to meet her for the purpose of having sexual intercourse. He was convicted of attempting to intentionally cause or incite a child under 13 to engage in sexual activity, contrary to the Sexual Offences Act 2003, s.8. The Court of Appeal upheld his conviction, applying the rule in *Shivpuri*.

Reforms

In its Report No. 276 on *Fraud* (2002), the Law Commission recommended that the crime of conspiracy to defraud should be abolished and that all offences of deception in the Theft Acts 1968–96 should be repealed and replaced with different offences. The Fraud Act 2006 effected the latter changes (see Ch.10 below). Abolition of the crime of conspiracy to defraud, however, has been deferred until there has been an opportunity to see how the new crimes in the Fraud Act work out in practice.

In its report No.300 *Inchoate Liability for Assisting and Encouraging Crime* (2006), the Law Commission recommended the abolition of the common law crime of incitement and the creation of two new inchoate offences: (i) encouraging or assisting the commission of an offence intending to encourage or assist its commission; (ii) encouraging or assisting the commission of an offence believing that it will be committed. The "encouraging" element would effectively replace the crime of incitement. These two new inchoate offences would catch someone who encouraged or assisted the commission of an offence which was then not actually committed. Thus the "assisting" element would fill the gap whereby at present someone who assists crime is not guilty as a secondary party unless the full offence is actually committed or attempted. For the Law Commission's proposals where someone encourages or assists an offence which is actually committed, see p.41 above.

6. GENERAL DEFENCES

As well as specific defences to particular crimes, there exists a number of defences available to all crimes. For the defence of consent, see p.94 below.

1. INSANITY

The mental fitness of the accused can be relevant in two contexts:

(i) *Unfitness to plead.* An accused may be found unfit to plead, if at the time the trial is to take place, he is found incapable of understanding the charge(s) and the pleas open to him and of following the evidence.

(ii) *Defence of insanity.* The accused may be found to have been insane at the time of the (alleged) commission of the offence. If successful, this defence results in a verdict of not guilty by reason of insanity.

The normal rule on the burden and standard of proof is that it is for the prosecution to prove that the accused is guilty and to do so beyond all reasonable doubt, *Woolmington v D.P.P.* (1935).

The House of Lords in that case recognised an exception in the case of insanity. Thus, where the accused claims he is unfit to plead or pleads the defence of insanity, it is for the accused to prove that he satisfies the requirements for such a finding and to do so on a balance of probabilities. Following the Criminal Procedure (Insanity) Act 1964 (as amended in 1991 and 2004), a finding of unfitness to plead or of insanity (other than in a murder case) does not involve the automatic making of an order committing the accused to a mental institution. The court has a range of responses available including: (i) an order committing the accused to a mental hospital with or without a restriction order; (ii) a supervision order; (iii) an absolute discharge.

The *M'Naghten* Rules

The requirements for a defence of insanity were first set out in the *M'Naghten* Rules which were the answers given by a panel of judges to questions which arose in Parliament following an insanity verdict in the case of *M'Naghten* who had killed the prime minister's private secretary. The Rules state that every man is presumed to be sane until the contrary is proved, and that to establish insanity:

> ". . . it must be clearly proved that at the time of the committing of the act the party accused was labouring under such a defect of reason, from disease of the mind, as not to know the nature and quality of the act he was doing; or, if he did know it, that he did not know he was doing what was wrong."

The accused has to show, on a balance of probabilities, that he satisfies the above test.

Disease of the mind

The legal definition of "disease of the mind" does not necessarily coincide with the medical definition.

Authority: *Kemp* (1957). D suffered from arteriosclerosis which caused him to have temporary blackouts. During one of these he attacked his wife with a hammer causing her grievous bodily harm. A disease of the mind was held to be any disease affecting the ordinary mental faculties of reason, memory and understanding, including for example, *Kemp's* arteriosclerosis. A disease of the mind can be temporary or permanent, curable or incurable.

Later cases have developed the definition further to include a range of illnesses which neither in medical nor everyday language would be classed as insanity.

Authority: *Sullivan* (1983). D had kicked and injured a man during an attack of psychomotor epilepsy. Medical evidence stated that this probably happened unknown to the accused during the third stage of an attack. The House of Lords held that epilepsy was a disease of the mind because D's mental faculties were impaired to the extent of causing a defect of reason. It was irrelevant that this was an organic disease which was only intermittent.

Authority: *Quick* (1973). D, a diabetic, injured a person while suffering from hypoglycaemia. The trial judge ruled that, having raised his state of mind as an issue in pleading automatism, D's only possible defence was insanity. D then pleaded guilty and appealed against the ruling. The Court of Appeal allowed the appeal and held that the blackout was caused, not by the disease (his diabetes), but by alcohol and lack of food combined with insulin. These were external factors and the temporary effect of the application of an external factor is not a disease of the mind and is not insanity. Diabetes, however, is a disease and if it is the cause of a blackout, that could amount to insanity.

Authority: *Hennessey* (1989). D was charged with taking a conveyance without authority and driving whilst disqualified. He was a diabetic who had been suffering from stress, and the stress had affected his blood sugar level and his requirement of insulin. His dose had therefore been inadequate and he had been suffering from hyperglycaemia. He pleaded automatism claiming that he was in a state of unconscious automatism, that he was hyperglycaemic at the time. The judge ruled that this, if true, amounted to insanity. The Court of Appeal upheld this ruling, holding that the hyperglycaemia was caused by an internal condition, diabetes, a disease of the mind. The stress and anxiety could not be treated as external causative factors. *Quick* was distinguished because hypoglycaemia is caused by external factors such as alcohol, food or too much insulin, and not by the diabetes itself.

Until 1991 sleepwalking was thought to be an example of automatism rather than insanity. Now, however, the courts treat sleepwalking as a disease of the mind with internal causes unless there is clear evidence of an external causal factor.

Authority: *Burgess* (1991). D committed an offence of violence while sleepwalking. The Court of Appeal held that the sleepwalking was caused by an internal factor and that the ordinary stresses and anxieties of life which may have triggered the sleepwalking were not sufficient to constitute an external factor.

Defect of reason

Once a disease of the mind is established it must be proved that it caused a defect of reason which had one of two consequences: *either* the defendant did not know the nature and quality of his act, *or* he did not know his act was wrong.

A defect of reason must be more than just a lapse of normal reasoning power in a stressful situation.

Authority: *Clarke* (1972). D was accused of theft from a shop. Her defence rested on forgetfulness due to depression. The trial judge held that this raised the issue of insanity and she changed her plea to guilty and then appealed. The Court of Appeal quashed her conviction saying that defect of reason implied a loss of reasoning power and not a mere temporary lapse due to forgetfulness.

(a) Nature and quality of the act

This covers the rare situation where the defendant, because of a defect of reason, does not understand the physical nature and quality of his act. Delusions as to the moral nature of his act do not excuse a defendant.

(b) Knowledge that the act was wrong

This has been held to mean legally, rather than morally, wrong.

Authority: *Windle* (1952). D killed his wife by an overdose of aspirin. Medical evidence was given that although he was suffering from a mental illness he knew that what he was doing was legally wrong. The Court of Appeal affirmed his conviction on the basis that the court cannot and should not make decisions as to moral rights and wrongs and can only decide what is contrary to law.

Court procedure

If the defendant puts his mental state in issue, e.g. by raising a defence of automatism or diminished responsibility, then the prosecution can raise the issue of insanity and bring evidence to prove it. In that case, the burden of proof rests on the prosecution to prove insanity beyond all reasonable doubt.

In certain circumstances, a verdict of manslaughter by reason of diminished responsibility can be returned by a jury instead of one of guilty of murder (see Ch.8). This has allowed defendants in a wide variety of circumstances involving mental impairment or disease, an alternative to the insanity defence.

Proposals for reform

The *M'Naghten* Rules are almost universally regarded as unsatisfactory, and reforms have been periodically suggested.

The most recent are those set out in the Law Commission's Draft Criminal Code, which adopts the recommendations of the Butler Committee, with some amendments. A jury would be able to return a verdict of not guilty on evidence of mental disorder, and the courts would have flexible disposal powers in responding to such a verdict. The verdict would be available either if all the act and fault elements of an offence were present but there was evidence of a severe mental illness or handicap which was relevant to the commission of the offence, or where fault could not be proved because of mental disorder.

2. AUTOMATISM

Automatism applies to the rare situation where the defendant is not legally insane but for some other reason is unable to control what he is doing. It can be explained either in terms of a lack of *actus reus*, as the act is not voluntary, or a lack of *mens rea*, because the defendant is not conscious of what he is doing.

The requirements for the defence of automatism are:

(i) the accused had a total absence of voluntary control over his actions;
(ii) that lack of control/unconsciousness was not due to a disease of the mind (in which case it would amount to insanity);
(iii) the automatic conduct was not self-induced (unless the crime charged is one of specific intent).

Automatism may occur for example when a defendant is in concussion, in a hypoglycaemic episode or in a hypnotic trance, provided that there is an external and not an internal cause. The external factor could be a traumatic event inducing severe shock. A good example is post-traumatic stress disorder, now increasingly recognised by the courts.

Authority: *T.* (1990). A few days after having been raped, D was involved in an incident which led to charges of robbery and causing actual bodily harm. Medical evidence showed that she was suffering from post-traumatic stress disorder and was not aware of what was happening. The court held that her state of mind was caused by the external event of the rape, and was therefore classed as automatism.

Authority: *Quick* (see above). D's conviction was quashed because the judge had ruled evidence of automatism inadmissible. The Court of Appeal said that such a situation was not insanity. It could give rise to a defence of automatism.

Self-induced automatism

Unless the crime charged is one of specific intent, automatism is no defence if the accused's automatic conduct was the result of the voluntary consumption of alcohol or dangerous drugs (otherwise than in accordance with a prescription) or if it was the product of recklessness by the accused. The accused will have been reckless if he realised that his actions or omissions (e.g. a diabetic's failure to take food when taking insulin) might render him liable to be aggressive, unpredictable, uncontrollable. Even in the absence of a prescription, however, taking drugs (e.g. valium) which are not generally known to be liable to lead to such behaviour will not deny the defence to the accused, unless he himself knew that they might lead to such behaviour.

Authority: *Bailey* (1983). D, a diabetic, attacked his ex-girlfriend's new boyfriend and injured him. He had felt unwell beforehand and had taken some sugar but no food. He suffered a hypoglycaemic episode during which he committed the assault. At trial the judge refused to allow evidence of automatism as his state was self-induced. On appeal the Court of Appeal held that on a charge of specific intent (e.g. under Offences Against the Person Act 1861, s.18), self-induced automatism can be a defence because it can negative the specific intent required for the offence. Further, in other crimes, it was held that self-induced automatism, other than that caused by the voluntary consumption of alcohol or drugs, can be a valid defence, unless the accused was reckless, *i.e.* knew that his acts or omissions (e.g. to take food) might render his conduct unpredictable, uncontrolled, aggressive.

For the rules relating to intoxication and the distinction between crimes of specific and basic intent, see the defence of intoxication, below.

Automatism and insanity—a comparison

A verdict of not guilty due to automatism leads to an acquittal. A verdict of not guilty by reason of insanity can lead to indefinite detention in a secure mental hospital or one of a range of other responses from the courts.

If a lack of voluntary behaviour is due to an outside factor, such as medication, a blow on the head or a traumatic event, a defence of automatism can succeed (*Quick, T.*), even if the automatism is self-induced (*Bailey*). If a lack of voluntary behaviour is due to an internal factor, this will be insanity (*Sullivan, Burgess*), even if the illness or condition is temporary and curable.

Where the accused pleads automatism, the burden to disprove it (beyond all reasonable doubt) falls on the prosecution. Where the accused pleads insanity, the burden to prove it (on a balance of probabilities) falls on the accused.

It is generally thought that automatism, since it is a denial of any voluntary action on the part of the accused, is a denial that the *actus reus* of the crime was present. Thus automatism is capable of being a defence to a crime which requires no *mens rea*, i.e. a crime of strict liability—see obiter in *Hill v Baxter* (1958). Insanity, on the other hand, is not available as a defence to a crime of strict liability, i.e. where *mens rea* is not in issue.

Authority: *DPP v H.* (1998). D was charged with driving with an excess of alcohol in his blood. The magistrates acquitted him on grounds of insanity after hearing evidence that he suffered from manic depressive psychosis with symptoms of distorted judgment and impaired sense of time and morals. The prosecution appealed. The Divisional Court acknowledged that insanity could be a defence to a summary offence, but held that it was a defence available only where *mens rea* is required as part of the offence. Therefore the court remitted the case to magistrates with a direction to convict.

3. MISTAKE

Mistake is not strictly speaking a defence, but a mistake or accident can negate liability if its effect is to negate the necessary *mens rea*. Although not a defence in the true sense, it is often considered along with, and overlaps, other defences.

Intention or recklessness

If the *mens rea* required is either intention or recklessness (see Ch.2), then any mistake which means that the defendant did not either intend an element of the *actus reus* or subjectively realise the risk involved, will be one which negatives *mens rea*. For example, if one element of the offence is lack of consent, and the requisite *mens rea* in relation to that element is subjective recklessness, then an honest mistake will negative *mens rea*, however unreasonable the mistake may be.

Authority: *Morgan* (1976). X and friends had been drinking. X encouraged his friends to have sexual intercourse with his wife saying that she would protest but would not mean it. They did so and ignored her protests. They pleaded not guilty to rape because they claimed that they had believed that she was consenting. The House of Lords said that an honest, albeit unreasonable, belief in the victim's consent would be enough to negate liability as *mens rea* would be missing. [The House of Lords in fact dismissed the appeal, because their Lordships were satisfied that the jury did not believe that the accused had made the mistake that they claimed to have made. Since the decision in *Morgan*, the definition of rape has been altered so that now a mistaken belief that the victim is consenting will be defence only if it is a reasonable mistaken belief: Sexual Offences Act 2003, s.1(1), p.91 below.]

Negligence

If an offence requires only negligence with regard to an element of the *actus reus* then *ex hypothesi*, only a mistake which is reasonable will negative the negligence.

Strict liability

If no *mens rea* is required with regard to one element of the *actus reus* then even an honest and reasonable mistake with regard to that element will not negative liability, *Bowsher* (1973)—see Ch.3.

Mistake as to an element of actus reus or of a defence

Generally a mistaken belief, whether reasonable or not, in the existence of any fact which if true would make the defendant's acts innocent, is a good defence: *B (a minor) v DPP* (2000) (Ch.3 above).

That general position is displaced where statute specifically requires the mistake to be reasonable. See, for example, the Sexual Offences Act 2003 in relation to a mistaken belief: (i) that the victim (e.g. of rape) is consenting, or; (ii) that a child (in the

case of crimes involving sexual activity with children under 16)
is over 16—pp.92–94 below.

Authority: *Williams (Gladstone)* (1983). D mistook his victim for a mugger attacking a youth and fought him off. His
victim was in fact a passer-by trying to arrest the youth who
had attacked and robbed a woman. D was charged with assault
occasioning actual bodily harm. He claimed that he had honestly believed his victim was assaulting the youth and that he
had been entitled to use reasonable force to prevent the crime
occurring. On appeal his conviction was quashed: the prosecution had to disprove the possibility that D had made an honest
mistake of fact. If a belief was honestly held, its unreasonable-
ness was irrelevant.

Authority: *Beckford* (1987). D was a policeman who had
shot and killed a suspect. His defence was that he had mistakenly believed his victim was about to shoot him. The Privy
Council on appeal held that D must be judged on the facts as he
mistakenly believed them to be, whether or not that was a
reasonable interpretation of them. D therefore had a defence of
self-defence, because the killing was not unlawful if, in the
circumstances as he perceived them to be, he had used reasonable force to defend himself.

It is important to remember that in relation to self-defence
and the prevention of crime there is still a requirement of
reasonableness as regards the amount of force used. An accused
can rely upon an unreasonable mistake as to when he can
defend himself, e.g. in unreasonably thinking himself to be
under attack or in thinking himself to be under a bigger attack
than he is. However, he is still entitled to use only *reasonable*
force, i.e. such force as is reasonably necessary to defend himself
from that perceived attack.

There is an exception to the rule that the accused can rely
upon an unreasonable mistake that he is under attack (or under
a bigger attack than he really is). The exception is that he cannot
rely upon a mistake arising from voluntary intoxication,
O'Grady (1987) and *O'Connor* (1991)—see "Intoxication" below.

Mistake of law

There is a general rule that ignorance of the criminal law is no
defence, even if the ignorance is reasonable in the
circumstances.

Mistakes which must be reasonable

The main offences where a mistake must be reasonable as well as honest are:

(a) Crimes of negligence.
(b) Statutory crimes which include a statutory defence such as "where the defendant believed, and had reasonable grounds to believe, that . . .".

Reforms

The Draft Criminal Code makes the following recommendations in respect of mistake; if a person believes in the existence of circumstances, he will have any defence he would have had if the circumstances had been as he thought. This applies a subjective test to mistakes as to circumstances. The Law Commission's latest proposals are in Report No. 218 (see p.79 below).

4. INTOXICATION

In some circumstances the defendant may not have the *mens rea* at the time he commits the *actus reus* because he is so intoxicated with alcohol or other drugs that he does not know what he is doing. Technically speaking this lack of *mens rea* should lead to an acquittal but strong policy reasons against this have led the courts to evolve a way of dealing with such cases which will normally lead to a conviction.

Voluntary intoxication is not strictly speaking a defence. However, it can negative *specific intent*, if it prevents the defendant forming the intent. In a crime of basic intent, if D was voluntarily intoxicated, it does not have to be proved that he actually had the *mens rea* (see *Majewski*, below). Instead, the test becomes: Would D, if he had been sober, have had the necessary foresight (the *mens rea*) for the crime in question? (*Richardson and Irwin*, 1999).

Authority: *D.P.P. v Majewski* (1976). D was involved in a fight while suffering from the effect of alcohol and drugs and unaware of what he was doing. The House of Lords held that evidence of voluntary intoxication cannot negative *mens rea* in a crime of basic intent. Although he was not aware of what he was doing, D could not be said to be acting involuntarily in the ordinary sense of the word and therefore he had the necessary basic intent.

Section 8 of the Criminal justice Act 1967, which says that an accused must not be taken as a matter of law to have intended the natural and probable consequences of his acts simply because they were natural and probable, has no application here. *Majewski* is based very firmly on policy and is difficult to explain in logical legal terms. It is based firmly on the notion that those who voluntarily take alcohol or dangerous drugs should realise the possible consequences in terms of violent behaviour and uncontrollable actions. In a loose sense they could be said to be reckless in taking the intoxicating substance and that recklessness suffices for the *mens rea* of a crime of basic intent. Thus the defendant's intoxication derived from alcohol or dangerous drugs voluntarily taken cannot be the basis of a defence to a crime of basic intent. However, the same rule does not, apparently, apply in the case of a drug, (e.g. a soporific one), not generally known to have, and not known to the accused to have, the potential of leading to violent, aggressive or unpredictable behaviour. That is so, even if the accused had not been prescribed the drug. In such a case the accused's intoxication is not itself a defence but it is relevant when the jury come to consider whether the accused was reckless.

Authority: *Hardie* (1984). D quarrelled with the woman he was living with and took some of her valium tablets to calm himself down. While under the influence of the drugs he set fire to the flat. His defence to a charge of criminal damage with intent to endanger life or being reckless as to endangering life was that he lacked *mens rea* due to the drug's effect. On appeal against conviction the Court of Appeal held that the usual rules regarding intoxication as a defence did not apply where the normal effect of the drug was soporific, and the jury should have been left to consider whether the defendant was reckless. See also *Bailey* and the other cases mentioned under Automatism above.

The rule in *Majewski* does not apply in the case of *involuntary* intoxication. Thus even where the crime charged is one of basic intent, the accused can rely on evidence of involuntary intoxication to show that he lacked the *mens rea* for the crime. However, if, despite the involuntary and blameless intoxication, D does have *mens rea*, he will still be liable.

Authority: *Kingston* (1994). D, who had paedophiliac tendencies, was convicted of indecent assault on a boy. He had admitted intending to carry out the act but claimed he would have restrained himself from doing so had he not been involuntarily drugged by another person. The House of Lords confirmed his conviction, holding that the absence of moral fault does not mean that there was no intent and the involuntary nature of the intoxication was only relevant if it caused a lack of *mens rea*. A drunken intent is still an intent.

Crimes of basic and specific intent

The distinction between crimes of basic intent and crimes of specific intent is particularly relevant to intoxication, since the rule in *Majewski* applies to the former and not to the latter.

Generally speaking, crimes of specific intent are crimes where a conviction cannot be obtained without proof of an intention whereas other crimes, including those where the *mens rea* is satisfied by proof of recklessness, are crimes of basic intent. Murder and all attempted crimes are crimes of specific intent. Another example is theft, the definition of which requires an *intent* permanently to deprive. Section 18 of the Offences Against the Person Act 1861 contains the crime of wounding or causing grievous bodily harm *with intent* to cause grievous bodily harm, etc. Some of these crimes require proof of intention or recklessness as to some circumstance, i.e. some other part of the *actus reus*. However, they all require proof of a particular intention and are thus crimes of specific intent. This approach does not, however, get the right answer in every case.

The only sure way to know which crimes are in which category is to learn the lists. Examples of crimes of specific intent are: attempts, murder, theft, (most forms of) burglary, wounding with intent.

Examples of crimes of basic intent are: common assault, assault occasioning actual bodily harm, malicious wounding or inflicting grievous bodily harm (contrary to s.20 of the Offences Against the Person Act 1861), rape, taking a conveyance without the consent of the owner, criminal damage, involuntary manslaughter.

Authority: *R v Heard* (2007). D was drunk. He undid his trousers, took his penis in his hand and rubbed it up and down the thigh of a police constable. He was charged with sexual assault contrary to the Sexual Offences Act 2003, s.3(1) (definition on p.91 below). One of the requirements of that offence is that the defendant "intentionally touches another person". D was convicted and appealed arguing that the jury should have been directed to consider whether his drunkenness meant that he did not have the intention to touch the constable. The Court of Appeal dismissed the appeal. For a conviction, the touching has to have been "deliberate". An accidental touching, even if objectively sexual, is not enough. To flail about, stumble or accidentally barge around in an uncoordinated manner, which results in a touching, would not suffice, even if that accident was caused by drunkeness. It is not, however, open to someone charged with sexual assault to contend that his voluntary intoxication prevented him from intending to touch. The offence is one of basic intent. In any case, on the evidence, D clearly did intend to touch the constable.

Voluntary intoxication for Dutch courage

If the defendant deliberately gets himself intoxicated in order to give himself the courage to commit an offence, which he subsequently commits when so intoxicated that it might be hard to prove he had the *mens rea* at that time, he will be unable to claim lack of intent, even in respect of a crime of specific intent.

Authority: *Attorney General for Northern Ireland v Gallagher* (1961). D decided to kill his wife. He brought a knife and a bottle of whisky which he drank to give himself Dutch courage. Then he killed her with the knife. The House of Lords held that he was guilty of murder and could not claim to have lacked intent or been insane.

Intoxication and defences

The defendant cannot rely upon voluntary intoxication to show, in relation to any crime, that he acted in a mistaken belief in the need to act in self defence or in prevention of crime. This rule applies equally to crimes of specific intent and to crimes of basic intent.

Authority: *O'Grady* (1987). D, because of intoxication, mistakenly thought he was being attacked by a friend and reacted violently, causing death. D was convicted of manslaughter and appealed against conviction, relying on the defence of self-defence in the circumstances as he mistakenly believed them to be. The Court of Appeal dismissed the appeal for the reason explained above.

This case evoked considerable criticism for its approach. It has, however, twice been confirmed in later cases in the Court of Appeal: *O'Connor* (1991) and *Hatton* (2005).

Authority: *O'Connor* (1991). D while drunk headbutted his victim, who died. D claimed he thought he was acting in self-defence. He was convicted of murder and appealed on the grounds that his mistaken belief was relevant. The Court of Appeal held (a) that his drunken mistaken belief could not found a defence of self defence but (b) that his voluntary drunkenness was relevant to the issue of whether he had the specific intent for murder. Since the judge had failed to direct the jury that voluntary intoxication might have prevented him having the specific intent to kill or to cause grievous bodily harm, his murder conviction was reduced to manslaughter.

The rule that the accused cannot rely upon his voluntary intoxication to support a claim that he mistakenly believed he needed to act in self defence is one which applies not only where the charge is one of basic intent but also where the charge is one of specific intent. This ruling in *O'Grady* and *O'Connor* has been heavily criticized. The Law Commission (Report No. 229–1995) recommends altering the law to allow the drunken mistake to be relied on where the offence charged requires proof of intention, purpose, knowledge, belief, fraud or dishonesty.

Authority: *Jaggard v Dickinson* (1981). D broke into a house which she thought belonged to a friend of hers who had given her permission to treat the house as her own. That mistake, though caused by voluntary intoxication, was enough to exculpate the defendant, by allowing her to rely on the statutory defence of lawful excuse under s.5(2) of the Criminal Damage Act. Because the test in s.5(2) is specifically set out in subjective terms, the court held that the reasons for a subjective belief in lawful excuse were irrelevant. Thus D was acquitted. This case is relevant only to the specific defence of lawful excuse under the Act and has no wider application.

5. PRIVATE DEFENCE

This term covers defence of oneself and others, defence of one's property, preventing crime and assisting lawful arrest. The defendant has a defence if he uses necessary and reasonable force in any of the above situations. This is controlled partly by common law (relating to self defence) and partly by s.3(1) of the Criminal Law Act 1967 (which allows the use of reasonable force in prevention of crime or in effecting, or assisting in, a lawful arrest).

Mistake

If the accused mistakenly believed himself to be under attack, or to have been under an attack bigger than it really was, then he is judged on the facts as he believed them to be—even if his mistake was an unreasonable one—see *Beckford* p.62 above. Thus, he is not guilty if he used force which was no more than reasonably necessary to defend himself from the attack he believed he was under. However, he cannot rely on his mistake if it was induced by voluntary intoxication, see *O'Connor* p.67 above.

Authority: *Scarlett* (1993). D was landlord of a public house and was forcibly ejecting a drunken customer. Believing that the customer was trying to attack him, he pinned his arms to his side and propped him up against a wall near some stairs. The customer fell down the stairs, hit his head and died. D was convicted of manslaughter on the basis of an unlawful act, namely that his actions against the customer were an assault. The Court of Appeal quashed the conviction, saying that it should have been made clear to the jury that he was not to be convicted if he had used no more than reasonable force in the circumstances as D had himself believed them to be.

Although the accused is entitled to be judged on the facts as he believed them to be (unless it was drunken mistake), he is not the arbiter of how much force it was reasonable to use in those circumstances. The test as to how much force is reasonable is an objective one for the jury to determine. The accused is not allowed to use as much force as *he* thought reasonably necessary. The question is whether he used more force than the jury considers was reasonably necessary to defend himself, *Owino* (1995).

Burden of proof

If the issue of self defence is raised, the burden of proof rests on the prosecution. Thus the accused is entitled to the benefit of the defence and to be acquitted unless the prosecution prove beyond all reasonable doubt that he was not acting in self defence or that he used more than reasonable force. The judge does not, however, have to direct the jury on the issue of self defence unless that issue is raised or there is some evidence on which it could be raised. If there is such evidence the burden of proof, as just stated, rests on the prosecution and the judge must direct the jury to consider the defence.

Reasonable force

A person can use only such force as is reasonable in all the circumstances, and it is up to the jury to decide whether the force used was reasonable. It is a question of fact not law. The jury must take into account such factors as the urgency of the situation, the ferocity of the attack, any other means open to the accused to defend himself such as retreating instead of using force and whether the accused's self defence had continued after the attack had ceased or the threat of attack had faded. Someone acting in self defence will often be doing so when faced suddenly with an attack or threatened attack. If, in the immediacy of the moment and without having time to weigh things to a nicety, the accused did what he honestly and instinctively thought was necessary, that is most potent evidence that the accused used only such force as was reasonably necessary, *Palmer* (1971). Similarly, it is not always necessary for the accused to have been attacked first and in some circumstances he may act pre-emptively to prevent an attack.

Authority: *Bird* (1985). D had been slapped and pushed by a man. She was holding a glass in her hand at the time and she hit out at the man in self defence without realising that she still held the glass. The trial judge directed the jury that self-defence was only available as a defence if the defendant had first shown an unwillingness to fight. The Court of Appeal quashed D's conviction saying that it was unnecessary to show an unwillingness to fight and there were circumstances where D might reasonably react immediately and without first retreating. It was up to a jury to decide on the facts of the case.

Authority: *Attorney General's Reference No. 2 of 1983*. It was held that it might, depending on the circumstances, be justifiable for a man to make and possess a petrol bomb where it was done to protect himself and his family from a threatened imminent attack. It could thus be a defence to a charge of possessing explosives. It would not be justifiable, however, if he continued to possess the bomb after the threat had passed.

Authority: *Martin (Antony) (2001).* D was being burgled by two people. He shot them, killing one. Rejecting his defence of self-defence, the jury convicted him of murder. He appealed, arguing that new evidence (that he had been suffering from a paranoid personality disorder) was relevant to the issue of whether the force used was reasonable. The Court of Appeal held that evidence of a defendant's psychiatric condition is not relevant to the issue of reasonable force, other than in exceptional circumstances making such evidence especially probative. The court did, however, reduce D's conviction to one for manslaughter on grounds of diminished responsibility.

Excessive force

If the defendant used more than reasonable force to defend himself, then he has no defence based on self defence. This is an "all or nothing" defence. The defence either succeeds so as to result in an acquittal or it is disproved in which case as a defence it is rejected. Thus on a murder charge, a finding that the accused acted in self defence but used excessive force means that the defence has been disproved. It does *not* result in a lowering of the verdict to a manslaughter verdict. Of course, the verdict may be reduced from murder to manslaughter on *other* grounds, such as provocation or lack of proof that the accused intended to kill or cause grievous bodily harm.

Authority: *McInnes (1971).* D was involved in a fight between two rival gangs. He had a knife and claimed (at his later trial for murder) that his victim ran on to it. He appealed against his conviction for murder arguing that the judge's direction on self defence was wrong in law. Dismissing the appeal, the Court of Appeal held that there was no provision for murder to be reduced to manslaughter on the grounds that the accused had acted in self defence but had used excessive force. The court pointed out the possibility of provocation reducing murder to manslaughter. The court also confirmed that there is no rule that for a successful plea of self defence the defendant must have retreated. The possibility of him retreating is simply a factor for the jury to take into account in deciding whether the accused used more force than was reasonably necessary.

Authority: *Clegg* (1995). D, a soldier, had fired at a stolen car being driven past him at a check point and killed a passenger. The House of Lords confirmed his conviction for murder because the trial judge had found as a question of fact that the amount of force used was unreasonable and excessive. Their Lordships confirmed the law established in *McInnes* and refused to bring about any change in the law by introducing a partial defence of self defence reducing liability to manslaughter, saying that that was a job for Parliament and not the courts, however desirable the change might be. [For the Law Commission's proposed reform of the law, see pp.120–121 below.]

6. DURESS BY THREATS

Duress covers the situation where the defendant is forced to break the law because of threats. It is a general defence available to all crimes with the exception of murder, attempted murder and, possibly, treason. The general rationale of the defence is that the criminal law should not demand a standard of resistance to threats which an ordinary reasonable person would find irresistible.

Duress as a defence to murder

Duress is no defence to murder or attempted murder. That is so irrespective of whether the defendant is alleged to be principal offender or secondary party.

Authority: *Howe* (1986). D and another person were involved in one murder as secondary parties. They were also principals to another murder and had conspired to kill a third person. They put forward duress as a defence, were convicted and appealed. It was held in the House of Lords that duress is no defence to murder when the accused is charged as principal offender. Their Lordships held also that duress was equally no defence to someone charged with murder as a secondary offender, thereby reversing the earlier decision of the House of Lords in *Lynch* (1975).

Authority: *Gotts* (1992). D attempted to murder his mother. His father had threatened to shoot him unless he did so.

His appeal against his conviction failed. The House of Lords held that duress is no defence to attempted murder.

In attempted murder, the existence of the threats can be taken into account when the judge is passing sentence. This is less true, however, in the case of murder where the judge has no option but to pass a life sentence, though the judge can take the threats into account in deciding what recommendation, if any, to make as to a minimum length of sentence to be served. Similarly, the Home Secretary can take such matters into account when deciding whether and when to release the murderer. The decisions in *Howe* and *Gotts* leave a question mark as regards the offence of wounding or causing grievous bodily harm with intent to cause grievous bodily harm. D may, for example, be scared by threats into an action, intended by him to cause grievous bodily harm. If that action results in the victim's death, the defendant has no defence of duress and is guilty of murder. If the action results, not in the victim's death, but only in the intended grievous bodily harm, is the defence of duress available? If so the defendant is not guilty. Similarly, what if the victim does not even suffer grievous bodily harm (e.g. the bullet or the knife misses or else it causes less than *grievous* harm)? Is the defence of duress available to attempting to cause grievous bodily harm? [The Law Commission has recommended allowing duress as a defence to murder and attempted murder, see p.79 below.]

Requirements for the defence

The requirements for the defence were laid down by the Court of Appeal in *Graham* (1982) and confirmed by the House of Lords in *Howe* (above). If the answer to both of the two following questions is yes, then the defence is made out:

(i) Was the accused impelled to act as he did because, as a result of what he reasonably believed to be the situation, he had good cause to fear that otherwise death or serious injury would result to himself or others, (e.g. his family)?
(ii) Would a sober person of reasonable firmness, sharing relevant characteristics of the accused, have responded as the accused did?

To found the defence, the threat of death or serious injury must be directed to the defendant, his immediate family or someone close to him or, very possibly, someone for whose safety the defendant would reasonably regard himself as responsible. The latter might include, where the defendant is a teacher, a threat directed at her pupils.

Duress is a true defence. The accused may have both committed the *actus reus* and had the *mens rea* for the crime charged but if the requirements above are satisfied, the defence succeeds and it results in an acquittal. Once duress is raised, the burden of proof rests on the prosecution to establish beyond all reasonable doubt that at least one of the requirements is not satisfied.

The second question is an adaptation of the "reasonable man" test in provocation. The characteristics to be attributed to the person of reasonable firmness can include the age and sex of the accused. Clearly, those characteristics which affect the gravity of the duress will also be attributed. For example, depending on the circumstances, pregnancy and serious physical disability could be relevant. Drug addiction, however, has been held to be a self-induced condition, not a characteristic, *Flatt* (1996). Also, it has been held that it is not a relevant characteristic that the accused was "extra pliable" or vulnerable to pressure, *Horne* (1994).

Authority: *Hegarty* (1994). D committed a robbery and claimed to have been subject to duress from persons who had threatened his family. He wanted to introduce medical evidence of his emotional instability and neurosis to show that he was particularly vulnerable to threats. The Court of Appeal held that emotional instability was not a relevant characteristic.

Immediacy and causal effect of the threat

Execution of the threat must be imminent and immediate, or reasonably believed to be so. Generally an opportunity to seek official protection, e.g. police protection, will preclude the accused having the defence. In *Hudson v Taylor* (1971) two teenage girls had committed perjury after having been threatened that, if they told the truth to the court, they would be "cut up". The Court of Appeal held that the threat had been sufficiently immediate to support a defence of duress, as their duressor had been present in court when they gave evidence and the threat could easily have been carried out in their home town that evening. This decision was disapproved in the House of Lords by Lord Bingham in *Hasan* (below). If the threat is not one which the defendant reasonably expects to be carried out immediately or almost immediately, the jury is likely to find that the defendant could have avoided committing the crime by going to the police or taking other evasive action.

The threat must have been a direct cause of the crime(s) with which the defendant is charged.

Authority: *Cole*   (1994).   Moneylenders   threatened "unpleasant consequences" to D unless he repaid his debt. In order to get the money he robbed a building society. The court recognised that there were two versions of duress: duress by threats and duress of circumstances. Denying him the defence on both versions, the court held that there must be a connection between the threat and the crime committed; those making the threats had not nominated the crime. Also, it was held, there had to be an imminent peril for the defence to succeed and here there had not been an imminent peril.

Voluntary exposure to duress

Where a defendant voluntarily associates with criminals who later exercise duress upon him to compel him to commit an offence, the defence will fail if the defendant foresaw, or ought to have foreseen, the risk of being subjected to threats of violence.

Authority: *R v Hasan* (2005 HL). D was a driver and minder for a woman who was involved in prostitution. The woman's boyfriend (F) also acted as her minder, was involved in illegal drugs and had a reputation for violence. D carried out an armed burglary. Charged with aggravated burglary, D said that F had threatened him with death or serious injury and had sent another individual to the burglary to see that D brought back the swag from the burglary. The judge directed the jury that D's defence of duress would fail if the jury found that, by associating with F, D had voluntarily exposed himself to the risk of being subjected to threats. In a wide review of the defence of duress, the House of Lords observed that duress is a defence easily pleaded and peculiarly difficult for the prosecution to disprove beyond all reasonable doubt. Where policy decisions had to be made, their Lordships were inclined to tighten rather than relax the conditions required for the defence to succeed. They held that the defence of duress is excluded when the defendant foresaw, or ought reasonably to have foreseen, the risk of being subjected to any compulsion by threats of violence as a result of voluntarily associating with others engaged in criminal activity. To deny the defence, it does not have to be shown that the defendant foresaw, or ought to have foreseen, the objective for which duress might be applied to him (e.g. to force him to commit an offence or to commit a particular type of offence). It is sufficient to show that he foresaw or ought to have foreseen that as a result of voluntarily associating with criminals, he might be subject to compulsion by threats of violence (whether to commit crimes or not). It is doubtful or undecided whether the same principle would apply to the following: (i) someone who voluntarily associates with a violent criminal for non-criminal purposes (e.g. by marrying the criminal); (ii) an undercover agent (e.g. a police officer) who penetrates a criminal gang for genuine law enforcement purposes and is later subject to the duress by the gang.

Mistake as to duress

Suppose that D claims that he believed, albeit mistakenly, that he was under duress or that the threats being applied were more serious than they really were. The defendant can rely only upon what he *reasonably* believed to be the situation. That rule, stated by the Court of Appeal in *Graham* and confirmed by the House of Lords in *Howe*, was re-confirmed by Lord Bingham in *Hasan*.

7. DURESS OF CIRCUMSTANCES

Threats can be made by another person or they can arise from the circumstances in which the defendant finds himself. Thus duress of circumstances is really the same defence as duress by threats—though it has sometimes been referred to as a defence of "necessity". The rules that apply are the same. Both are concerned with threats of death or serious injury which overbear the will of the defendant. The requirements for the defence to succeed are the same. Just like duress by threats, so equally duress of circumstances is available not just in driving cases but to offences generally, i.e. apart from murder and attempted murder. As regards murder see *Dudley and Stephens* (p.78 below).

Authority: *Martin* (1989). D was charged with driving whilst disqualified. His defence was that he had a suicidal wife who had threatened to kill herself if he did not drive their son to school. On appeal his conviction was quashed. The court held that his defence of duress should have been left to the jury to consider, applying the rules established in *Graham* (1982). See also *Cole* (p.74 above).

Authority: *Pommell* (1995). D was charged with having possession of a firearm without a licence. He claimed that a man had visited him at 1 a.m. and that D had persuaded the man to leave with D the loaded gun which the man had been carrying with the intention of shooting some people later on. The police had found D in possession of the gun at 8 a.m. later the same morning when executing a search warrant at D's premises. On those (assumed) facts the Court of Appeal held that D had the defence of duress for his initial possession of the gun. Whether he had that defence for his continued possession until 8 a.m. depended on whether the jury considered that in not contacting the police earlier he had failed to desist from committing the crime as soon as he reasonably could.

Authority: *Abdul-Hussain* (1999). The Ds were Iraqis living in Sudan and fearing being deported back to Iraq. They boarded as passengers, and later hijacked, an aircraft from Sudan bound for Jordan. It landed 12 hours later at Stansted. Charged with hijacking, they pleaded duress of circumstances, i.e. they feared death at the hands of the authorities if they were returned to Iraq. The trial judge ruled that the threat was insufficiently immediate to amount to duress. The Court of Appeal held that to be too restrictive a view and allowed their appeals against conviction. The execution of the threat need not be immediately in prospect. There had to be an "imminent" peril operating on the defendants' minds so as to impel them to act as they did—though the amount of terror to innocent passengers raised issues of proportionality, i.e. whether a sober person of reasonable firmness would have reacted as the defendants did. [The correctness of this decision is doubtful, after the emphasis given by the House of Lords in *Hasan* to the requirement that the threat must be both immediate and imminent.]

Authority: *R v Quayle, Attorney General's Reference (No 2 of 2004)*. Ds were charged with various offences concerned with cultivation, possession, use, importation and supply of cannabis. Three of the Ds suffered from very painful conditions resulting from such things as amputations and accidental injuries. Each believed his activities in producing or possessing cannabis were necessary to avoid him suffering unnecessary pain. Two other Ds had imported or possessed cannabis in order to supply it in a clinic to persons for whom they regarded themselves as responsible and who they feared would otherwise suffer serious pain. The Court of Appeal held that the defence of "necessity by circumstances" was subject to the same rules, set out in *Hasan*, as apply to duress by threats. It was not available to any of the Ds for two reasons: (i) the necessitous use of cannabis for pain relief was in conflict with the legislative scheme for controlling the use of drugs; (ii) the cases being appealed did not involve any imminent and immediate risk of serious injury, a risk of pain alone being insufficient to found a defence of duress or necessity.

Authority: *R v Jones* (2006). The Ds committed acts of civil disobedience and criminal damage at RAF air bases. Charged with offences, including criminal damage, they claimed that they had been trying to prevent the impending attack on Iraq. They advanced three defences: (i) that they were using reasonable force under Criminal Law Act 1967, s.3 to prevent a crime (the international crime of aggression); (ii) lawful excuse under Criminal Damage Act 1971, s 5(2)(b); (iii) duress/necessity of circumstances. Dismissing these defences, the Court of Appeal held that duress/necessity of circumstances is a domestic defence to a domestic crime. It is available when the defendant commits an otherwise criminal act to avoid an imminent threat of death or serious injury to himself or persons for whom he reasonably regards himself as responsible. The Ds would have difficulty showing that they reasonably regarded themselves as responsible for the people of Iraq. On a further unsuccessful appeal, the House of Lords held that the focus of the Criminal Law Act 1967, s.3 is entirely domestic and cannot make lawful activity undertaken to prevent the international crime of aggression which is not a crime in English Law.

8. NECESSITY

Duress of circumstances has in the past sometimes been characterised as "necessity": prison officers held entitled to force feed prisoners in order to save their lives, *Leigh v Gladstone* (1909); doctor held entitled to carry out abortion for the purpose of saving the life of the mother, *Bourne* (1939). In more recent times the "necessity" tag has been used to describe, for example, the situation where someone seizes another and forcibly drags him from the path of an oncoming vehicle, thereby saving him from injury or even death, *per* Lord Goff in *Re F* (1990). It may be that all these examples are really cases of a defence of necessity distinct from the defence of duress, since they are not cases of a defendant's will being overborne, i.e. being forced to act against his will. Rather, the circumstances were so compelling that the defendant felt—and most normal people would feel—that he ought to act the way he did. Even before the defence of duress was judicially recognised, the courts had been reluctant to allow the defence of necessity to a charge of murder.

Authority: *Dudley and Stephens* (1884). Ds, after being ship-wrecked and without food and water for several days, killed and ate a third member of their crew. They were convicted of murder, though the death sentence was subsequently commuted to six months' imprisonment. The judgment denied the defence of necessity. For Lord Coleridge C.J., if there was to be such a defence, it would be impossible to choose which of the crew was to die and "Who is to be the judge of this sort of necessity? By what value is the comparative value of lives to be measured?" and the defence "once admitted might be made the legal cloak for unbridled passion and atrocious crime".

Where, however, fate has already "designated" one individual for death, the defence may be allowed—for example where D is roped to a climber who has fallen, whom D cannot rescue and who, unless D cuts the rope, will pull D to his death.

Authority: *Re A (conjoined twins; surgical separation)* (2000). M and J were conjoined twin babies. J was capable of independent existence but M was not. M was alive only because a common artery enabled J to circulate oxygenated blood for them both. If there were no operation to separate them, both would die, probably within three to six months. If there were an operation, it would enable J to lead a normal life but would inevitably result in the death of M. The parents wished there to be no such operation. The Court of Appeal held the operation would be lawful because:

(a) the doctors owed conflicting duties to J (to carry out the operation to preserve her life) and to M (not to kill her) and the law had to resolve that conflict by allowing the lesser of two evils;

(b) since M was draining J's life-blood, killing M was justified by a defence of "quasi" self-defence;
(c) the three requirements for the defence of necessity were satisfied.

These were:

(i) the act (the operation) was needed to avoid inevitable and irreparable evil (death of J within six months);
(ii) no more should be done than was necessary for the purpose to be achieved; and
(iii) the evil inflicted (death of M) was not disproportionate to the evil avoided.

9. PROPOSALS FOR REFORM

The Law Commission has published several papers in this area.

Intoxication

The Law Commission's Report No. 229 (1995) on *Intoxication and Criminal Liability* recommends no newly created defence, but a codification of existing law, based on *Majewski*. This is seen as the most practical and workable of a variety of solutions considered. The same principle would govern voluntarily induced automatism. See also *O'Connor* (p.67) above for the Report's recommendation about a drunken mistake in relation to self defence.

Duress by threats and duress of circumstances

The Law Commission Report No. 218 (1993) on *Offences Against the Person and General Principles* recommends that duress, both by threats and of circumstances, be extended to all crimes (including murder) but that the burden of proof be shifted to D to prove his defence on a balance of probabilities. He would not have a defence if he had knowingly or unreasonably exposed himself to the risk of the threat. See also the Law Commission Report No 304 (2006), *Murder, Manslaughter and Infanticide*, p.119 below.

The justifiable use of force

The Report's recommendations on private defence would allow D to use such force as is reasonable in the circumstances as he believes them to be, but he would not be able to rely on any circumstances of which he was unaware, and the Report lists the instances where the use of force is deemed to be in public or private defence.

7. NON-FATAL VIOLENCE OFFENCES

The main non-fatal violence offences, other than sexual offences, are common law assault and battery and the aggravated assault offences under the Offences Against the Person Act 1861, ss.47, 20 and 18.

Certain offences are more serious and carry heavier penalties, if they are racially aggravated. They are: assault; battery; the offences in ss.47, 20 and 18 of the 1861 Act; criminal damage (see Ch.10 below) and the offences of harassment (p.89 below). An offence is racially aggravated if it is motivated by hostility towards members of a racial group or if, at the time of the offence, the defendant demonstrates racial hostility towards the victim: Crime and Disorder Act 1998, s.32.

1. ASSAULT AND BATTERY

In criminal law, as in civil law, assault and battery mean different things, although the word "assault" is sometimes used to cover both.

Thus in *Kimber* (1983) it was said:

> "An assault is an act by which the defendant intentionally or recklessly causes the complainant to apprehend immediate, or to sustain, unlawful personal violence."

Assault and battery are now summary offences covered by s.39 of the Criminal Justice Act 1988.

Actus reus of assault

The essence of assault is that the victim is put in fear. The *actus reus* of assault can be committed by acts or words or a combination of both. It is now established that words alone can give rise to an assault. The House of Lords has held that even the making of silent telephone calls is capable of amounting to an assault: *Ireland, Burstow* (1997) (see p.86 below). Whether it is the words or acts of the defendant or a combination of both which are in issue, there will be no assault unless they cause the victim to apprehend the immediate infliction of violence. A threatening gesture which the victim does not observe cannot be an assault upon him. On the other hand, the victim does not have to be sure that violence will definitely be inflicted or that it will definitely be inflicted immediately. It is enough that the victim apprehends that it *might* be inflicted and that it *might* be inflicted immediately.

Authority: *Constanza* (1997). D stalked his victim over a period of two years. He followed her home from work, made numerous silent telephone calls, sent over 800 letters, visited against her express wish and wrote offensive words on her front door. He sent her two letters which she interpreted as threats. She believed that he might do something to her at any time and was diagnosed as suffering from clinical depression. He appealed against his conviction for an assault occasioning actual bodily harm, arguing that there had been no assault (a) because a victim can have no fear of immediate violence unless the victim can see the alleged assailant, and (b) an assault cannot be committed by words alone. Dismissing the appeal, the Court of Appeal held that both these arguments were wrong. This case was decided before the House of Lords decision in *Ireland, Burstow* (below) but is entirely consistent with it. It seems clear that a telephone call can amount to an assault where it causes the victim to apprehend personal violence in the immediate future.

Authority: *Arobieke* (1987). D had been following his victim and was looking at a train which he thought his victim might have boarded. His victim was not on the train but panicked when he saw D and tried to escape across a railway line. The line was live and the victim was electrocuted. The court held that D was not guilty of unlawful act manslaughter because his actions did not constitute an assault. There was no apprehension by the victim of the immediate infliction of violence.

Mens rea of assault

The *mens rea* of assault is a subjective one. It is satisfied by proof of intention or of *Cunningham* recklessness. Thus the defendant has the *mens rea* of assault if he intends the victim to apprehend the immediate infliction of personal violence or else he foresees that the victim might do so. For *Cunningham*, see Ch.2. The subjective nature of the test for *mens rea* in assault was confirmed by the House of Lords in *Savage, Parmenter* (1991), see p.87 below.

Actus reus of battery

The *actus reus* of battery is the slightest "direct" application of force to another person. It is sufficiently direct if done via a medium controlled by D, e.g. D sets his dog on V or throws a brick which hits V. When D punched a mother causing her to drop her child who hit his head on the floor, this was a battery upon the child (as well as upon the mother): *Haystead v D.P.P.* (2000). A battery has been said to require a hostile act, but in the House of Lords in *Re F* (1990) Lord Goff said:

> "I respectfully doubt whether that is correct. A prank that gets out of hand; an over-friendly slap on the back; surgical treatment by a surgeon who mistakenly thinks that the patient has consented to it—all these things may transcend the bounds of lawfulness, without being characterised as hostile. Indeed the suggested qualification is difficult to reconcile with the principle that any touching of another's body is, in the absence of lawful excuse, capable of amounting to a battery and a trespass."

As to lawful excuse, his Lordship recognised that consent can be a defence to assault and also made the following observations:

> "There are also specific cases where physical interference without consent may not be unlawful—chastisement of children, lawful arrest, self-defence, the prevention of crime, and so on . . . [A] broader exception has been created to allow for the exigencies of everyday life—jostling in a street or some other crowded place, social contact at parties, and such like. This exception has been said to be founded on implied consent, since those who go about public places, or go to parties, may be taken to have impliedly consented to bodily contact of this kind. Today this rationalisation can be regarded as artificial; and in particular, it is difficult to impute consent to those who, by reason of their youth or mental disorder, are unable to give their consent. For this reason, I consider it more appropriate to regard such cases as falling within a general exception embracing all physical contact which is generally acceptable in the ordinary conduct of everyday life."

The *actus reus* of a battery can be a continuing act.

Authority: *Fagan v Metropolitan Police Commissioner* (1969). D had driven his car on to a policeman's foot by mistake but was slow to remove it when he realised what he had done. The

court held that the *actus reus* of the battery was the remaining on
the foot and the intention then formed to remain was sufficient
mens rea.

Mens rea of battery

The *mens rea* of battery is satisfied by proof of intention or of
Cunningham recklessness. Thus to have the *mens rea* of battery,
the defendant must intend to apply force to another or else
foresee that his actions might result in the application of such
force.

Defences to Assault and Battery

For the defence of consent see p.94 below. For the general
defences of self defence, duress, etc., see Ch.6. Corporal punishment in schools, both state schools and private schools is now,
by statute, no longer permitted. Reasonable chastisement for the
purpose of correction by a parent is compatible with the
European Convention on Human Rights provided the jury is
directed to take into account the following five factors when
deciding whether the chastisement was reasonable:

   (i)   the nature and context of D's behaviour;
   (ii) its duration;
   (iii) the physical and mental consequences for the child;
   (iv) the age and personal characteristics of the child;
   (v)   the reasons D gives for the punishment. (*R v H* (2001))

The Children Act 2004, s.58 now provides that the defence of
reasonable chastisement is not available to a charge under ss.18,
20 or 47 of the Offences Against the Person Act 1861, nor to a
charge under the Children and Young Persons Act 1933, s.1
(cruelty to someone under 16). The defence remains available to
a charge of assault or battery.

2. OFFENCES AGAINST THE PERSON ACT 1861

Section 47

This section makes it an offence, punishable with a maximum of
five years imprisonment, to commit "an assault occasioning
actual bodily harm". The word "assault" here is used to mean

either an assault or a battery. Thus for the s.47 offence there has to be actual bodily harm which is caused by either an assault or a battery. There will be no assault or battery unless the *actus reus* of the assault or battery was accompanied by the *mens rea* (i.e. for the assault or battery). Thus for the s.47 offence, the following two elements are required:

(i) Either (a) the *actus reus* plus the *mens rea* of assault or (b) the *actus reus* plus the *mens rea* of battery.
(ii) Actual bodily harm caused by the assault or battery.

The *mens rea* required is the *mens rea* for the assault or battery. No *mens rea* is required as to the causing of actual bodily harm—see *Savage, Parmenter* (p.87 below). Thus there is no need to prove that the defendant foresaw any bodily harm.

The *actus reus* for the crime is: both (a) the *actus reus* of assault or of battery, and (b) the causing of actual bodily harm by that assault or battery. The *actus reus* requires there to be a causal link between the assault (or battery) and the actual bodily harm, the test of causation being an objective one of whether the actual bodily harm was a foreseeable consequence of the defendant's action. Thus, an action of the victim which is so daft or so unexpected that no reasonable person could be expected to foresee it, would break the chain of causation—see *Roberts* (p.5 above). Actual bodily harm includes any personal injury whether or not it is serious. A cut or bruising could qualify as actual bodily harm. Cutting off a substantial part of someone's hair can amount to actual bodily harm (though consent would be a defence): *DPP v Smith* (2006). Also included is psychiatric injury, though not mere emotions such as fear, distress or panic nor psychological symptoms which do not amount to a recognised psychiatric illness.

Authority: *Chan Fook* (1994). D acted aggressively towards his victim and locked him in an upstairs room. The victim's evidence was that he felt abused, humiliated and frightened. D was convicted of an assault occasioning actual bodily harm. The Court of Appeal held that actual bodily harm could include psychiatric injury, though not mere emotions such as fear, distress and panic. The only evidence of psychiatric harm in this case, however, had been that of the victim and D's conviction was quashed because where psychiatric injury is alleged as the actual bodily harm, expert evidence must always be called.

Otherwise, the issue should be withdrawn from the jury. This case has since been approved by the House of Lords in *Ireland, Burstow* (below).

Section 20

Under this section:

> "Whosoever shall unlawfully and maliciously wound or inflict any grievous bodily harm upon any other person either with or without any weapon or instrument shall be guilty of an offence . . .".

The *actus reus* for s.20 is either wounding or inflicting grievous bodily harm. Wounding involves a complete break in the skin. A graze will be insufficient for a wound unless the skin is completely broken, *McLoughlin* (1838). Similarly, a broken collar-bone is not a wound unless the skin is broken. It could, however, amount to grievous bodily harm. Grievous bodily harm means really serious bodily harm, *D.P.P. v Smith* (1961). There is no real difference between "really serious bodily harm" and "serious bodily harm", *Saunders* (1985). As long it is "serious" or "really serious", psychiatric harm will satisfy the definition—though where psychiatric harm is the basis of the charge, expert evidence must be called.

Authority: *Ireland, Burstow* (1997). The appeals in two different cases were heard together by the House of Lords. In *Ireland*, D had made a lot of unwanted telephone calls to three women—sometimes repeated calls over a short period. When the women answered there was silence. According to expert evidence the effect of the calls was in each case that the women suffered significant psychological symptoms including palpitations, cold sweats, anxiety, insomnia, dizziness and stress. D was convicted on three counts of an assault occasioning actual bodily harm and appealed, eventually, to the House of Lords. In *Burstow*, D refused to accept that a woman wished to end the relationship he had had with her. Over a six-year period he followed her to work, repeatedly visited her house, turned up unexpectedly at places where she happened to be. He sent her hate mail, stole clothing from her washing line and scattered condoms in her garden. As a result she suffered endogenous depression with marked features of anxiety. He was convicted of maliciously inflicting grievous bodily harm contrary to s.20

and appealed, eventually, to the House of Lords. Both appeals were dismissed. It was held:

(i) that bodily harm in ss.47 and 20 included a recognisable psychiatric illness (approving *Chan Fook*, p.85 above);

(ii) the word "inflict" in s.20 was capable of embracing someone inflicting psychiatric injury upon another—one can inflict grievous bodily harm under s.20 without any physical violence being applied to the victim's body, either directly or indirectly;

(iii) making silent telephone calls causing psychiatric injury, whilst not capable of amounting to a battery, was capable of amounting to an assault and therefore could form the basis of a charge under s.47.

In *Ireland, Burstow*, the House of Lords has made it clear that serious bodily harm can be "inflicted" with or without there being any assault and that it can be "inflicted" without there being even any personal violence at all, whether direct or indirect. Statements to the contrary in earlier cases are no longer good law. See also *Dica*, p.95 below.

The *mens rea* for s.20 is denoted by the word "maliciously". This indicates that the *mens rea* is satisfied by proof of either intention or *Cunningham* recklessness. It is not necessary, however, for the defendant to intend or foresee bodily harm of the seriousness required for the *actus reus* of this offence. Whereas the *actus reus* requires the defendant to wound or to inflict "serious" bodily harm, the *mens rea* is established by proof that the defendant intended or foresaw bodily harm. It is not necessary for the prosecution to prove that the defendant intended or foresaw that the bodily harm would be serious: *Mowatt* (1968). The test is a subjective one requiring proof that the defendant intended or foresaw bodily harm, albeit not necessarily serious bodily harm: *Grimshaw* (1984).

Authority: *Savage, Parmenter* (1991). Appeals in two separate cases were heard together in the House of Lords. In *Savage*, D threw a glass of beer at her victim. In the process D lost a grip of the glass itself which broke and cut the victim's wrist. D was convicted of inflicting grievous bodily harm contrary to s.20. On appeal to the Court of Appeal this was reduced to a conviction for an assault occasioning actual bodily harm contrary to s.47. D appealed to the House of Lords against this conviction, arguing that she had not foreseen that her action might cause any bodily harm. In *Parmenter*, D had caused damage to the bone structure of his baby son. At his trial on a charge that D had maliciously inflicted grievous bodily harm, contrary to s.20, the judge directed the jury that he was guilty if he *should* have foreseen some bodily harm, even if only of a minor nature. The Court of Appeal quashed the resulting conviction because the jury should have been directed not to convict unless sure that D had actually foreseen some bodily harm. The Court of Appeal refused, however, to substitute a conviction for an assault occasioning actual bodily harm contrary to s.47. The prosecution appealed against that refusal. The House of Lords dismissed D's appeal in *Savage* and allowed the prosecution's appeal in *Parmenter*. Their Lordships held: (i) there is a subjective test for the *mens rea* for the offence in s.20 which requires proof that the defendant foresaw the risk of causing some bodily harm; and (ii) the *mens rea* required for an assault occasioning actual bodily harm contrary to s.47 is the same as that for common assault, (i.e. for an assault or a battery) and for s.47 the prosecution does not have to prove that the defendant intended or foresaw any bodily harm.

Section 18

This section provides:

> "Whosoever shall unlawfully and maliciously by any means whatsoever wound or cause any grievous bodily harm to any person, with intent to do some grievous bodily harm to any person, or with intent to resist or prevent the lawful apprehension or detainer of any person, shall be guilty of an offence . . .".

The *actus reus* requires a "wound" or the causing of "grievous bodily harm". These expressions have the same meaning as in s.20. Under s.18 the defendant must have *caused* grievous bodily harm as opposed to *inflicted* it. However, after the decision of the House of Lords in *Ireland, Burstow* (p.86 above), there seems little, if any, difference between *causing* something and *inflicting* it.

On a charge of wounding or causing grievous bodily harm with intent under s.18, an alternative verdict of guilty of maliciously inflicting grievous bodily harm contrary to s.20 is possible. This will be relevant if the jury are not satisfied that D had the necessary intent for a conviction under s.18 but are satisfied that D foresaw the risk of at least some bodily harm.

The *mens rea* required for the offence in s.18 is an intention. One of the following forms of intention must be proved:

(i) an intent to cause grievous bodily harm, or
(ii) an intent to resist or prevent a (lawful) arrest or detention.

The offence is thus, unlike the offences in ss.20 and 47, one of specific intent, which is relevant where the defendant is voluntarily intoxicated—see p.63 above. Nothing less than intention will suffice.

Authority: *Belfon* (1976). D attacked his victim with a razor causing him serious injury. He was charged with wounding with intent to cause grievous bodily harm. The judge directed the jury that he had sufficient *mens rea* if he foresaw that his actions would probably cause serious injury. He appealed. The Court of Appeal held that under s.18, recklessness was not sufficient *mens rea* and that an intention to cause grievous bodily harm had to be proved. The court therefore quashed D's conviction under s.18 and substituted a verdict of guilty under s.20.

Turning to the alternative intention, it appears to be enough *mens rea* that D intended to resist an arrest which was in fact lawful, i.e. even if D believed it to be unlawful: *Lee* (2000). D would, however, have the defence of self-defence if he used no more force than was reasonably necessary to resist an arrest which, though in fact lawful, was unlawful on the facts as D mistakenly believed them to be: *Blackburn v Bowering* (1994).

3. HARASSMENT

In 1996/7 a number of cases arose which involved the modern phenomenon of stalking, i.e. persistently pursuing someone (sometimes a lover who had jilted the accused or someone who had rebuffed the accused's sexual advances). In some of these cases the accused was charged with assault, or with offences under ss.18, 20 or 47 of the Offences Against the Person Act 1861. Some of these eventually resulted in the definitions of the offences being judicially widened—see *Constanza* (p.82 above) and *Ireland, Burstow* (p.86 above). In the meantime Parliament was legislating to make stalking a crime. The result was the Protection from Harassment Act 1997. It created two new offences:

Harassment. It is an offence to pursue a course of conduct which amounts to harassment of another and which the accused knows, or ought to know, amounts to harassment (ss.1 and 2). The statute provides no definition of harassment beyond stating that it includes alarming or causing distress. This is a summary offence punishable with a maximum of six months imprisonment. As few as two incidents can amount to a course of conduct, but only if there is a sufficient connection between them: *Lau v D.P.P.* (2000). The incidents which comprise the course of conduct (e.g. repeated abusive phone calls) could occur within a period as brief as five minutes: *Kelly* (2003). A course of conduct could be classed as a single offence of harassment even though directed at more than one person, provided those persons were a close knit definable group (e.g. man and wife) living in the same house and the conduct was clearly aimed at each one on each occasion, even though only one might have been present on any one occasion: *DPP v Dunn* (2000).

Putting the victim in fear of violence. A person whose course of conduct causes another to fear, on at least two occasions, that violence will be used against him commits an offence under s.4 if he knows or ought to know that his course of conduct will cause the other to fear violence against him on each of those two occasions. The maximum sentence is five years imprisonment.

It is not enough that D frightened or even "seriously frightened" his victim. The offence is not committed unless the victim feared violence would be used against the victim: *Henley* (2000). A threat of violence to the victim's family or her dog could form the basis of a prosecution, provided that (a) it caused the victim to be put in fear of violence being used against the victim and (b) D knew or ought to have known that it would cause such fear: *R. v D.P.P.* (2000) (where a threat in the presence of the victim to blow out her dog's brains caused her to fear violence to herself).

4. RAPE AND OTHER SEXUAL OFFENCES

The Sexual Offences Act 2003 swept away most of the earlier offences controlling sexual activity, including: rape; indecent assault; sexual intercourse with girls under 13 or 16; abduction; incest. It replaced them with a range of over 50 offences, which prohibit broadly the same range of activity. The names of some former offences are no longer used, e.g. indecent assault and incest, and some former offences (e.g. abduction) have no direct replacement. Significant changes were made in relation to mistake as to consent (e.g. in rape) and mistake as to age (i.e. in offences against a child under 16).

Offences requiring lack of consent

Three offences are defined respectively in s.1(1), s.2(1) and s.3(1) of the Sexual Offences 2003:

Rape

1. (1) A person (A) commits an offence if—

   (a) he intentionally penetrates the vagina, anus or mouth of another person (B) with his penis,
   (b) B does not consent to the penetration, and
   (c) A does not reasonably believe that B consents.

Assault by penetration

2. (1) A person (A) commits an offence if—

   (a) he intentionally penetrates the vagina or anus of another person (B) with a part of his body or anything else,
   (b) B does not consent to the penetration, and
   (c) A does not reasonably believe that B consents.

Sexual assault

3. (1) A person (A) commits an offence if—

   (a) he intentionally touches another person (B),
   (b) the touching is sexual
   (c) B does not consent to the touching, and
   (d) A does not reasonably believe that B consents.

The offence in s.3(1) is an offence of basic intent, see *Heard* (2007), p.65 above.

Section 4 makes it an offence to cause someone (B) to engage in sexual activity without consent.

Consent

For the purposes of the four above offences, "a person consents if he agrees by choice, and has the freedom and capacity to make that choice", s.74. In these offences, a mistaken belief that B is consenting will amount to a defence only if it is a *reasonable* belief. That is different from

    (a) what the law on rape previously was (see *Morgan*, p.61 above), and

    (b) the position in relation to offences outside this Act (e.g. common assault) where consent is a defence (see *Aitken*, p.95 below).

It is no longer the law that a woman is taken to have consented to sexual intercourse simply by virtue of being the defendant's wife: *R* (1992).

Sections 75 and 76 set out evidential and conclusive presumptions regarding consent. These sections apply to the four offences (in the 2003 Act) mentioned above but do not apply to offences outside the Act where consent is a defence. Unless evidence is adduced to the contrary, B is taken, in the specified circumstances, not to have consented and the accused is taken not have reasonably believed that B consented (s.75). The specified circumstances are where:

- at the time of (or immediately before) the relevant act any violence was used against B (or anyone else) or B was caused to fear that it was being used or would be used, or;
- at the time of the relevant act: B was asleep or unconscious; B was (and the accused was not) unlawfully detained; B was, due to physical disability, unable to communicate consent or lack of consent, or; there had, without B's consent, been administered to (or caused to be taken by) B a substance capable of causing B to be stupefied or overpowered.

It is conclusively presumed that B did not consent and that the accused did not believe that B consented, in the situation where the accused intentionally deceived B as to the nature or purpose of the act or intentionally induced B to consent by impersonating someone known personally to B (s.76).

"Penetration is a continuing act from entry to withdrawal" (s.79). Thus, where during intercourse, the defendant realises that the B is not, or is no longer, consenting, then any subsequent continuation of intercourse will amount to the offence, even if until that point no offence had been committed. This is similar to the law prior to the Sexual Offences Act 2003: *Kaitamaki* (1984). For the general common law on consent, see p.94 below.

Sexual offences against under-aged persons

The offences in ss.5 to 8 are exactly the same as the offences in ss.1 to 4, respectively, except that

(a) these latter offences are committed when B (the victim) is aged under 13, and
(b) B's consent is no defence.

For the offences in ss.5 to 8, there is no defence of mistaken belief as to either age or consent.

Authority: *R v G* (2006). D appealed against his conviction for rape of a girl under 13, contrary to Sexual Offences Act 2003, s.5. He claimed that, himself a 15 year old, he had believed her to be 15, i.e. over 13. He appealed arguing that because the offence in s.5 did not allow a defence based on such a belief, it was incompatible with Art.6(2) of the European Convention on Human Rights (which states the presumption of innocence). The Court of Appeal held that there is no incompatibility with Art.6 where a statute creates a strict liability offence, thus imposing liability in the absence of blameworthiness. Art.6 is concerned not with the definition of a crime but with the fairness of the criminal process.

Sections 9 and 10 create the offences of sexual activity with a child under 16 (s.9) and causing a child under 16 to engage in sexual activity (s.10). In each case:

(i) consent of the victim is no defence;
(ii) if the child victim is under 16, the defendant is not guilty if he *reasonably* believed the victim to be over 16;
(iii) there is no defence of mistaken belief as to age, if the child victim is under 13.

The requirement that the defendant's belief (that the victim is over 16) must be reasonable is a change to what the law previously was—see *B v DPP* (2000) and *R v K* (2001), p.23 above.

5. CONSENT

Crimes can for this purpose be divided into two categories: (i) crimes, such as rape and assault, where the consent of the victim means that the *actus reus* of the offence is not complete; (ii) crimes, such as murder and offences involving sexual activity with a child under 16, where consent is no defence. Normally, an assault which is intended to cause, or which does cause, actual bodily harm is in the latter category. For specific provisions relating to consent in rape and other sexual offences, see the Sexual Offences Act 2003 (p.90 above).

Authority: *Brown* (1993). Ds were involved in a series of sadomasochistic sexual acts in private. They all consented. During these activities the Ds inflicted injuries on each other. They were convicted of offences under ss.47 and 20 of the Offences Against the Person Act 1861, and appealed on the grounds that the victims' consent made the actions lawful. The House of Lords held that all assaults causing more than merely transient harm will be unlawful, even if they are consented to, unless there are good policy reasons for allowing the consent to operate.

Exceptional cases where consent is a defence even though actual bodily harm is caused include: lawful sports, dangerous exhibitions, reasonable surgical interference, tattooing. Consent can be a defence where actual bodily harm is caused during rough horseplay. Consent can also validly be given to the risk of serious infection during consensual sexual intercourse.

Authority: *Barnes* (2004). During an amateur football match, D injured another player in what the prosecution alleged was a late, unnecessary, reckless and crushing tackle. D appealed against his convictions under ss.20 and 47 of the Offences Against the Person Act 1861. The Court of Appeal held that a foul, even if sufficient to justify a sending off, is not necessarily outside the scope of the consent impliedly given by other players. The jury should have been directed to determine whether D's action was within what could be anticipated in a normal game of football or was something quite outside it.

Authority: *Wilson* (1996). D's wife asked him for a tattoo as she wanted his name on her body. So, with a knife and with her consent, he burnt his initials onto her buttocks. His conviction was quashed. The Court of Appeal held that, since what the accused did was no more dangerous than tattooing and public policy did not demand that the activity should be criminal, the defence of consent was available on those facts.

Authority: *Aitken* (1992). During celebrations some RAF officers drank a lot of alcohol and indulged in horseplay which included setting alight the fire resistant suit of an officer who was wearing it. He was severely burnt. The culprits were convicted of maliciously inflicting grievous bodily harm. The convictions were quashed on appeal. The Court of Appeal held that if the victim had consented, or if the defendants had believed (whether or not reasonably) that the victim was consenting, to their activities, that was a defence.

Authority: *R. v Dica* (2003). D, who knew that he was HIV positive, had consensual sexual intercourse, unprotected, with two different women with each of whom he had a long term relationship. Each of the women subsequently tested positive for HIV. D was charged with two offences of maliciously inflicting grievous bodily harm, contrary to s.20 of the Offences Against the Person Act 1861, by recklessly infecting each of the women with HIV. The prosecution's case was that neither woman would have agreed to sexual intercourse (protected or unprotected) with him, if she had known that he was HIV positive. **Held**: (i) recklessly infecting the victim can amount to the offence in s.20 and *Clarence* (1889) was no longer good law; (ii) D was not guilty of rape since each of the women had consented to sexual intercourse; (iii) given the long term nature of the relationships, if D had concealed the truth about his HIV condition with the result that either of the women was unaware of the risk of infection, then she was not consenting to that risk and consent would be no defence to the charge under s.20; (iv) if either of the women had known about D's HIV positive condition, then consent to run that risk would be a good defence to the charge under s.20—unlike consent to the deliberate and intentional infliction of bodily harm for the purposes of sexual gratification which did not amount to a valid defence in *Donovan* (1934), *Brown* (1994), *Boyea* (1992) and *Emmett* (1999).

Consenting victim makes a mistake

Consent is no defence where it is vitiated (negatived) by mistake. This will be the case where the victim's mistake (whether or not induced by fraud) is as to either (i) the identity of the accused or (ii) the nature and quality of the act consented to. Thus consent is no defence where D has sexual intercourse with the victim whose consent he has gained by impersonating her husband/boyfriend/partner. Nor is consent a defence where the victim is mistaken as to the nature and quality of the act (e.g. thinks it is not sexual intercourse but a medical procedure). Consent is not, however, negatived by other mistakes: e.g. that D is wealthy man or that D would pay her £25 for sexual intercourse (*Linekar* 1995). There are now, however, specific statutory provisions in relation to consent in sexual offences—see the Sexual Offences Act 2003 (p.92 above).

Authority: *Richardson* (1999). D, a disqualified dentist carried out dental treatment on patients who were unaware that she was disqualified. D was not guilty of assault. The patients' consent was not negatived by their mistake which was not a mistake as to D's identity or as to the nature and quality of the act consented to.

[The Law Commission, in its report *Consent in Sex Offences* (2000), recommended *Richardson* be reversed by a statutory provision that a person's identity is capable of including his professional qualification—a recommendation not implemented in the Sexual Offences Act 2003.]

Authority: *Tabassum* (2000). D got several women to take part in a cancer survey he was carrying out in order to prepare a software database to sell to doctors. This involved them removing their bras and allowing D to feel their breasts. They consented to this but would not have done so if they had known D not to be medically qualified. It was held that this mistake as to the "quality" of his act negatived their consent and that he was guilty of indecent assault. *Tabassum* seems inconsistent with earlier cases, including *Richardson*. If *Tabassum* is correctly decided, then consent can be negatived by a mistake as to either:

   (i) the identity of the accused, or
   (ii) the *nature of* the act, or
   (iii) the *quality* of the act.

[In relation to sexual offences, the Sexual Offences Act 2003, s.76 now creates a conclusive presumption that there was no consent where the defendant intentionally deceived the victim as to the *nature* or *purpose* of the act—see p.92 above].

True consent

Consent induced by fear is not a true consent. However, the fact that the victim does not physically retreat, does not mean that the victim consents. Mere submission is not the same thing as consent—see *Day* (1841) where a 10–year-old girl who had offered no resistance to an adult man was held not to have consented. Similarly there is no need for evidence of the use of force by the accused, i.e. to overcome resistance from the victim. Thus it is possible for an accused to rape a victim while she is asleep, unless of course she gave her consent before falling asleep, *Larter and Castleton* (1995). In relation to the victim of an alleged sexual assault being at the time asleep or unlawfully detained or in fear of violence etc, see the evidential presumptions in the Sexual Offences Act 2003, s.75 (p.92 above).

Authority: *Olugboja* (1981). D threatened to keep a girl in his home overnight, though he made no explicit threats of violence and she did not resist sexual intercourse. It was held that on the evidence she had not consented but had merely submitted to intercourse under the pressure of his threat.

Reforms

The Home Office consultation paper, *Violence—Reforming the Offences Against the Person Act 1861* (1998) made clear the Government's intention to reform the 1861 Act along the lines proposed in the Law Commission Report No. 218 (1993). The Government was not yet ready, however, to consider the wider reforms proposed by the Law Commission, e.g. of the law relating to duress and the use of justifiable force. (For those wider reforms see p.79 above.) According to the draft Offences Against the Person Bill attached to the Home Office paper, the main offences in the 1861 Act (i.e. ss.18, 20 and 47 and some others) would be replaced with the following new offences:

  (i) intentionally causing serious injury (max: life imprisonment).
 (ii) recklessly causing serious injury (max: seven years).
(iii) intentionally or recklessly causing injury (max: five years).
 (iv) causing serious injury with intent to prevent or resist lawful arrest (max: life imprisonment).
  (v) committing an assault with intent to prevent or resist arrest (max: two years).

Throughout the draft Bill, intention and recklessness are given consistent meanings, the definitions of both involving a subjective test. The draft Bill would also replace the common law crimes of assault and battery, with a statutory crime of assault reproducing those same crimes in statutory form. Also included in the draft Bill were crimes dealing with: assault on a constable; dealing with explosives; threatening death or serious injury; administering a substance capable of causing injury. The draft Bill has never been introduced into Parliament.

8. HOMICIDE

Homicides are unlawful killings. The major categories are murder and manslaughter. Others include corporate manslaughter and causing or allowing the death of a child or vulnerable adult.

1. MURDER

Murder, a common law offence, is the unlawful killing of a human being under the Queen's peace with malice aforethought.

Actus reus

The killing must be of a human being. The unlawful killing of an unborn child therefore is not murder and is covered by other offences. On the other hand, if injuries are inflicted on an unborn child which is then born alive and subsequently dies of the pre-natal injuries, that can amount to murder, *Attorney General's Reference No. 3 of 1994* (see p.19 above).

"Under the Queen's peace" means that the killing of an enemy in the course of war will not be murder.

The killing must be unlawful. Certain defences (see Ch.6), for example self-defence, will make a killing lawful.

The requirement that the death must occur within a year and a day of the defendant's action was abolished by the Law Reform (Year and Day Rule) Act 1996. However, no proceedings may be commenced without the consent of the Attorney General if either the injury which is alleged to have caused the death occurred more than three years before the death or the defendant has previously been convicted of an offence alleged to be connected with the death.

It is, of course, necessary for the prosecution to establish that the defendant caused the death. For cases on causation see Ch.1.

Mens rea

The *mens rea* for murder has traditionally been described as "malice aforethought". This expression is now inappropriate since both words are misleading. The accused does not have to have acted maliciously, i.e. out of malice. Nor does the accused have to have premeditated the killing. The *mens rea* of murder is established by proof that the accused had, at the time he carried out the act which caused the death, either (i) an intention to kill or (ii) an intention to cause grievous bodily harm.

Before 1957, there was a third alternative—which was termed constructive malice. Thus it used to be sufficient for the prosecution to establish that the killing occurred whilst the defendant was committing a crime of violence, *D.P.P. v Beard* (1920). Constructive malice was abolished by the Homicide Act 1957.

The possibility remains that someone can be convicted of murder despite having no intention to kill and despite not even foreseeing that death might occur—provided that he intended grievous bodily harm. Over the years there has been criticism of this. It has been suggested that the *mens rea* required for murder should be limited to an intention to kill, (see for example the minority speeches in the House of Lords in *Cunningham* (1981)). It is now, however, generally accepted that abolition of the alternative strand (an intention to cause grievous bodily harm) is a matter for the legislature. Until the legislature changes the law, the two strands of *mens rea* remain and thus an intention to cause grievous bodily harm is sufficient *mens rea* for murder. [For the Law Commission's proposed reforms, see p.119 below.]

Foresight of consequence

At one stage it seemed that a person was deemed to have the intention to kill or to cause grievous bodily harm if that was a natural consequence of his actions. This is very definitely not now the case. Intention is a subjective matter. Section 8 of the Criminal Justice Act 1967 provides that a person is not to be taken as intending the natural and probable consequences of his act simply because they were natural and probable, but a jury must consider all the evidence before deciding whether they are satisfied that *he* had the necessary intention. For the current law on the meaning of "intention", see *Moloney, Shanklin and Hancock, Nedrick* and especially *Woollin*, all set out in Ch.2.

2. VOLUNTARY MANSLAUGHTER

There are two main kinds of manslaughter: voluntary and involuntary manslaughter.

Voluntary manslaughter covers the situation where the defendant has the necessary *actus reus* and *mens rea* for murder but is able to rely on one of three particular defences. Those three defences are:

(i) provocation,
(ii) diminished responsibility, and
(iii) killing in the course of a suicide pact.

If any one of these defences is successful, it does not result in an acquittal. It merely reduces what would be murder to manslaughter. The practical difference this achieves is that the accused is convicted of a crime, manslaughter, which does not quite carry the public stigma of a murder conviction and the judge has a discretion as to what sentence to impose. A murder conviction leaves the judge no option but to pass a life sentence whereas a manslaughter conviction allows the judge to pass any sentence up to life imprisonment. These three defences are then defences only to murder. On the other hand, in the case of any other crime, the judge can in sentencing take into account any mitigating factor such as provocation, etc.

Provocation

Under s.3 of the Homicide Act 1957:

> "Where on a charge of murder there is evidence on which the jury can find that the person charged was provoked (whether by things done or by things said or by both together) to lose his self-control, the question whether the provocation was enough to make a reasonable man do as he did shall be left to be determined by the jury; and in determining that question the jury shall take into account everything both done and said according to the effect which, in their opinion, it would have on a reasonable man."

For the defence to succeed there are thus three requirements:

(i) There must have been some act(s) or word(s) of provocation.
(ii) The defendant must have lost his self control.
(iii) The circumstances must be such that a reasonable man would have reacted as the defendant did.

The defendant does not have to prove these requirements. If there is some evidence of provocation, the judge must leave the issue of provocation to the jury and that is so irrespective of whether the accused actually pleads provocation. That could for example arise if the accused pleads self defence, perhaps where the prosecution argues that the evidence shows that the accused went "over the top" in his reaction to being attacked and used excessive force. This may suggest that the attack caused the accused to lose his self control. The judge will, of course, direct the jury to consider the defence of self defence which the accused raised, but should also direct them to consider provocation. If he does not and the jury convict of murder, his failure to direct the jury on provocation is a ground of appeal. If on the other hand, there is no evidence of what was said or done which could have amounted to provocation, the judge does not have to direct the jury on provocation.

Authority: *Rossiter* (1992). D was a victim of domestic violence over a period of years. In response to an attack by her husband which was not life threatening, she lost control and stabbed him many times, killing him. Her defence of self defence was rejected by the jury who convicted her of murder. On appeal, the Court of Appeal held that, under s.3 of the Homicide Act 1957, it had been the duty of the judge to put the issue of provocation to the jury, even though it had not been raised by the defence. There was evidence on which the jury might have found that she lost her self control and that a reasonable woman might have reacted in the way she did. Therefore her conviction for murder was quashed and a conviction for manslaughter substituted. (There is no similar rule in relation to diminished responsibility requiring the judge to direct the jury on that defence where the accused does not raise it, *Straw* (1994).)

Authority: *Cambridge* (1994). D's defence to a murder charge was that he was not the attacker at all, and he therefore did not raise provocation as a defence, although there was relevant evidence. His appeal against conviction was allowed because the judge should have put the possible defence before the jury.

Authority: *Acott* (1997). D's mother was found dead after having consumed a lot of alcohol and after having received multiple injuries. D's defence, on a charge of murder, was that his mother's injuries had been the result of an accidental fall. In cross examination it was suggested to D that he had inflicted her injuries and killed her having lost his temper, perhaps after they had had a row or because of her drinking, or because she was becoming more difficult, or because she treated him like a child. The judge did not direct the jury to consider the defence of provocation. Dismissing D's appeal, the House of Lords held that the judge had not been under a duty to direct the jury to consider the defence of provocation because there had been no evidence as to what the provocation in this case was. In the absence of any such evidence it would be impossible for the jury to determine if D was provoked or, if he was, whether a reasonable man would have reacted in the same way.

The provocation will usually have come from the deceased with whose murder the accused is charged. There is, however, no requirement that this be so.

Authority: *Davies* (1975). D was jealous of his wife's relationship with another man, S. After certain earlier incidents, on this occasion he spotted S walking towards the library where D's wife worked. He followed S there and shot and killed his wife as she came out to meet S. On a plea of provocation, the judge directed the jury to consider the whole course of the wife's conduct and decide whether D had been provoked to kill her. Allowing his appeal, the Court of Appeal held that the judge should have directed the jury to consider not just the wife's acts but also those emanating from a source (here S) other than the victim.

Did the defendant lose his/her self control?

The defendant has to have suffered sudden and temporary loss of self control. This is often an immediate response to the provocation. However, immediacy of loss of self control is not a requirement. The issue is whether it was the provocation which caused the loss of self control; the closer they are in time, the more likely is the jury to conclude that it was. In some cases there is evidence that the accused suffered a history of provocation such that the eventual alleged loss of self control could have been when the accused suddenly "snapped". In such a case, the judge must in the summing up to the jury, not only review that evidence but must analyse the various strands of provocation.

It used to be thought that there was a requirement that the accused's actions must be proportionate to the provocation.

This, however, is not a requirement. If in fact the accused's response was disproportionate, then that is a factor for the jury to consider when deciding the actual question which is: Did the accused suffer a sudden temporary loss of control? (Of course, disproportionality of response will also be a factor for the jury to take into account when deciding the reasonable man test, below.)

The question of whether the accused lost his self control is a subjective one. The burden of proof rests on the prosecution. The jury must decide this issue in favour of the accused, if they think that the accused *may* have acted in a moment of loss of self control because of the provocation.

Authority: *Ahluwaliah* (1992). D had set fire to her husband while he was asleep. She had been the victim of domestic violence for many years but her response to her husband's violence was not *immediately* following any specific act of his. The Court of Appeal held, inter alia, that there must be a sudden and temporary loss of self control but that it need not follow immediately upon the provocation. On this particular point the judge had, however, not made any misdirection.

Authority: *Humphries* (1995). The deceased had raped, beaten and terrorised D for a period of time. He had threatened her on the night she killed him. Allowing her appeal against conviction for murder, the Court of Appeal held that the deceased's behaviour to D over a long period of time should have been reviewed by the judge in the summing up and the judge should have analysed the different strands in the history of provocation suffered by D.

The "reasonable man" test

The second element of the provocation test is objective. The jury must decide whether a "reasonable man" would have acted as the defendant did.

Authority: *D.P.P. v Camplin* (1978). D, a 15-year-old boy, hit a 50-year-old man over the head and killed him. D's defence was provocation. He claimed the deceased had forcibly buggered D and then had laughed at him whereupon D lost his self control and fatally attacked the deceased. The judge directed the jury (as to whether the alleged provocation was enough to make a reasonable man act as D had done) to consider the effect the alleged provocation would have had on an adult man. The House of Lords reduced D's murder conviction to manslaughter. Their Lordships held that the judge ought to have directed the jury to consider the effect the alleged provocation would have had on a person of the same sex and age as D, i.e. upon a 15-year-old boy,—i.e. would it have been enough to make a reasonable 15-year-old boy react as D had done? It was held that the "reasonable man" means a person having the power of self control of an ordinary person of the sex and age of the accused and in other respects sharing such of the accused's characteristics as would affect the gravity of the provocation.

Authority: *Morhall* (1995). Over some hours the deceased criticised D for his addiction to glue sniffing. The deceased then voiced this criticism again and also head-butted D. A fight between them ensued, was broken up and then resumed again which was when D stabbed and killed the deceased. D appealed against his conviction for murder on the ground that the jury should (in relation to his defence of provocation) have been directed to consider whether a reasonable man who was addicted to glue sniffing would have reacted in the way D had done. Allowing his appeal and substituting a manslaughter verdict for his murder conviction, the House of Lords held that D's addiction to glue sniffing should have been attributed to the reasonable man since it was something which affected the gravity of the provocation in this case.

After *Morhall* there arose a conflict of authorities over the extent to which characteristics of the accused which reduce the accused's level of self control are to be attributed to the reasonable man. On the one hand, the Privy Council held that a defendant's mental infirmity, such as brain damage, (or other individual peculiarity) which impaired or reduced his powers of self control should not be attributed to the reasonable man, *Luc Thiet Thuan* (1996). The reasoning was that if characteristics of the accused reducing his powers of self control were to be attributed to the reasonable man, that would remove the objective element in the reasonable man test. On the other hand, in *Smith (Morgan James)* (2000), the House of Lords held that, in considering whether the reasonable man would have reacted the way D did, the jury may take into account not only D's age and sex but also D's other characteristics, including those which reduce D's ability to exercise self control. This conflict was resolved by the decision in *Attorney General for Jersey v Holley*.

Authority: *Attorney General for Jersey v Holley* (2005). D, a chronic alcoholic, killed his girlfriend with an axe whilst he was drunk. At his trial for murder the sole issue was provocation. The judge directed the jury that the fact that a person was under the influence of alcohol at the time of the killing and as a result he was provoked more easily than if he were sober, is not something to be taken into account in his favour when determining if a reasonable person would have reacted as he did. The Privy Council upheld that approach. A particular characteristic of D (such as mental infirmity, clinical depression, drunkenness, alcoholism or where D suffers from battered wife syndrome, post-natal depression, personality disorder) may be relevant to two issues, namely: (i) whether D lost self control, and, (ii) the gravity of the provocation to D. On this latter issue, the decision in *Morhall* (1995) had been correct. The House of Lords decision in *Smith (Morgan James)* had, however, been wrong. The objective standard of self-control by which D's conduct is to be evaluated does not vary from defendant to defendant. It is the external standard of a person exercising the ordinary powers of self-control of someone of D's age and sex. The reasonable person is not to be invested with any particular characteristic of D other than D's age and sex. The reasonable man test requires the jury to decide whether, having regard to the actual provocation and their view of its gravity for D, a person of D's age and sex and having ordinary power of self-control might have done what D did. [Although three of the nine judges dissented, this case has settled English law on this issue until Parliament sees fit to change it by legislation: *R v James, R v Karimi* (2006).]

Self-induced provocation

If the defendant induces the provocation by some act of his own then it is much more difficult to rely on provocation as a defence, and the provocation must be extreme compared with the original act for the defence to apply, but provocation is not automatically unavailable as a defence simply because it is self-induced.

Authority: *Johnson* (1989). V and D had been drinking. D used threatening behaviour towards V, and V used insulting words and behaviour towards D. A struggle developed resulting in the death of V. D pleaded reasonable self defence, because he thought he would be hit by a glass. He was convicted of murder, and appealed on the grounds that the judge should have left the issue of provocation to the jury. The Court of Appeal substituted a manslaughter verdict. The fact that the provocation which caused D to lose his self control was the predictable result of D's own actions did not mean that provocation should not be put to the jury. It should have been. The jury would then have been able to decide whether a reasonable man would have reacted to the provocation in the way the accused did.

Diminished responsibility

If a defendant can prove on a balance of probabilities a defence of diminished responsibility, he will be guilty of manslaughter rather than murder. Section 2(1) of the Homicide Act 1957 states:

"Where a person kills or is party to the killing of another, he shall not be convicted of murder if he was suffering from such abnormality of mind (whether arising from a condition of arrested or retarded development of mind or any inherent causes or induced by disease or injury) as substantially impaired his mental responsibility for his acts and omissions in doing or being a party to the killing."

Abnormality of mind

An abnormality of mind is a state of mind which the reasonable man would consider abnormal. It is therefore defined very widely and covers many conditions which are not covered by the insanity defence.

Authority: *Byrne* (1960). D had strangled his victim and then mutilated her body. He claimed he was subject to an irresistible or almost irresistible impulse because of perverted sexual desires which overcame him and had done so since he was a boy. The Court of Appeal quashed his conviction for murder because the trial judge had misdirected the jury that s.2 of the 1957 Act was irrelevant here. The court said that the defence covered the mind's activities in all its aspects and the ability to control one's physical acts. This would cover the irresistible impulse situation.

Abnormality of mind has been held to cover severe shock or depression common in mercy-killing cases and "battered wife syndrome." (See *Ahluwalia* (1992).)

How the abnormality arises

This covers:

(i) A condition of arrested or retarded development of mind.
(ii) Any inherent causes.
(iii) Disease or injury.

Abnormality of mind induced by alcohol or drugs is not generally due to inherent causes and thus does not come within the definition. It can, however, include disease which has been caused by long term drug or alcohol consumption.

Authority: *Gittens* (1984). D suffered from depression and had been in hospital. On a visit home he had an argument with his wife and he clubbed her to death. He then raped and killed his stepdaughter. He had been drinking and taking drugs for medication. The Court of Appeal held that in such a case the jury has to discount the effect of the alcohol and drugs and to decide whether the combined effect of the inherent causes, (i.e. without the effect of the alcohol and drugs) amounted to such abnormality of mind as substantially impaired his mental responsibility at the time.

This ruling was approved in *Dietschmann* (2003) where the House of Lords held that the jury must *not* be directed to consider the question "Would D have killed if he had not taken alcohol?" but simply to consider, as in *Gittens*, whether the combined effect of factors falling within s.2(1) (e.g. psychopathic tendencies, retarded mental development, but excluding the effect of any alchohol D had consumed) amounted to such abnormality of mind as had substantially impaired his mental responsibility.

Authority: *Tandy* (1987). D was an alcoholic. On this particular day she had drunk much more than normal, and she strangled her daughter. She did not claim that she could not stop herself from drinking, and admitted that she was able to exercise some control over her drinking initially. The judge withdrew the diminished responsibility defence from the jury. D appealed, but the appeal was dismissed. The court held that the abnormality of the mind which resulted in the killing had to be induced by the alcoholism in order for the defence to apply. In order for the craving of alcohol to produce the abnormality of mind, it must be such as to render the use of alcohol involuntary, and this was not the case here, as D admitted having some control over whether she had that first drink. The defence should therefore not be left to the jury in such circumstances.

Authority: *Inseal* (1992). D killed his girlfriend while he was drunk and claimed that alcoholic dependency syndrome was relevant to his diminished responsibility defence. The court held that brain damage, psychosis or alcoholic dependency syndrome, if caused by alcoholism, could all be diseases of the mind, but there was a difference between that and the situation where D has become less inhibited because of a large intake of alcohol and that particular drinking bout has caused him to commit the act. (The same point was made concerning paranoid psychosis caused by drug taking in *Sanderson* (1994).)

The effect of the abnormality of mind

The abnormality of mind must substantially impair the defendant's mental responsibility. The impairment therefore need not be total. The defendant may know what he is doing, know it is wrong, and have some control over himself but find it substantially *more* difficult than a normal person would to control his actions. This difficulty in controlling himself must be caused by the abnormality of mind.

Authority: *Byrne* (see above). The evidence in the case was not that D found the impulse irresistible but that he found it very difficult to control. This suffices under the 1957 Act.

Diminished responsibility and insanity—relationship & burdens of proof

Insanity is a general defence to all crimes (except possibly those of strict liability, see *D.P.P. v H* at p.60 above). If the defence of insanity succeeds, it results in a special verdict, "Not guilty by reason of insanity". Diminished responsibility is a defence only to murder and if successful reduces what would be a murder conviction to one of guilty of manslaughter. Thus, on a murder charge, either defence can be advanced. Diminished responsibility as a concept is wider than insanity. If both defences are advanced and insanity is proved, then the correct verdict is an insanity verdict. Where the accused pleads diminished responsibility or insanity the burden of proof rests upon the accused to establish the defence on a balance of probabilities. It could occur, however, that the accused pleads diminished responsibility and it is the prosecution which argues that insanity is the proper verdict. In that case, the prosecution has the burden of proving insanity beyond all reasonable doubt. If the prosecution fails to do that, then the court will have to decide whether the accused has established that it is more likely than not that he was affected by diminished responsibility.

Authority: *Lambert, Ali and Jordan* (2000). Article 6.2 of the European Convention on Human Rights sets out the presumption of innocence. Section 2(2) of the Homicide Act 1957 places upon the defendant the burden of proving diminished responsibility. The Court of Appeal held that s.2(2) does not violate Art.6.2 of the Convention, because s.2(2) relates to a "special defence or exception" intended for the benefit of defendants and Parliament has specifically placed the burden of proof on the defendant.

Suicide pacts

Section 4 of the Homicide Act 1957 provides:

> "(1) It shall be manslaughter and shall not be murder for a person acting in pursuance of a suicide pact between him and another to kill the other or be a party to the other being killed by a third party."

The burden of proof rests on the accused to establish the defence on a balance of probabilities, s.4(2). This reverse legal burden of proof is not incompatible with the European Convention on Human Rights: *Attorney General's Reference (No.1 of 2004)*.

Note that the Suicide Act 1961 abolished the crime of suicide and, with it, the crime of attempted suicide. By virtue of that same 1961 Act, however, it is still an offence to aid, abet, counsel or procure suicide, confirmed by the House of Lords in *The Queen on the application of Dianne Pretty v D.P.P.* (2001). Section 4 of the Homicide Act 1957, however, deals with the situation where the accused is charged, not with attempting his own suicide (now no longer criminal) nor with aiding or abetting another suicide, but with murder. This could, for example, occur where the accused and another agree that they both intend to die and pursuant to that agreement, they lock themselves in a room, each take sleeping pills and the accused turns on the gas tap. A rescuer breaks down the door by which time the accused has not, but his partner has, succumbed to the lack of oxygen and died of asphyxiation.

3. INVOLUNTARY MANSLAUGHTER

Involuntary manslaughter is the term given to an unlawful homicide where the necessary *mens rea* for murder is not present. There are two main kinds of involuntary manslaughter: unlawful act manslaughter, and manslaughter by gross negligence.

Constructive (or unlawful act) manslaughter

D is guilty of constructive manslaughter if:

   (i) he has committed an unlawful act,
  (ii) the unlawful act was dangerous, and
 (iii) the unlawful act caused the death.

Unlawful act

To be an unlawful act for the purpose of constructive manslaughter, the act must amount to a crime. However, not all crimes are unlawful acts for this purpose. Thus an activity, (e.g. driving) which is lawful but which can become criminal only by virtue of the negligent or careless way it is carried on does not amount to an unlawful act even if it is carried on in that way. Even in the case of a crime which does not fall within the latter category, (e.g. assault), there is no unlawful act unless the *crime* is committed. Thus, it is not an unlawful act to commit the *actus reus* of the crime unless the *mens rea* is also present. Nor is it an unlawful act if the accused has a defence such as consent or self-defence.

    Authority: *Andrews v D.P.P.* (1937). D had been driving dangerously and knocked over and killed a pedestrian. He was convicted of manslaughter. The House of Lords held that careless driving was a lawful act done with a degree of carelessness sufficient to make it a statutory offence. It was not an unlawful act for the purposes of manslaughter. It followed that for a manslaughter conviction, the prosecution had to establish gross negligence. (For the lesser offences of causing death by dangerous driving and causing death by careless driving, see p.119 below.)

Authority: *Lamb* (1967). D and his friend were playing with a revolver. Knowing that there were bullets in two of the chambers and also that neither bullet was in the chamber opposite the barrel, D thus believed that the gun would not fire. He failed to realise that, on the trigger being pulled, the cylinder of chambers would automatically rotate. He aimed it and fired it at point blank range at his friend, who was killed. He was charged with manslaughter. The judge directed the jury that the accused had committed an unlawful act even if he had not intended to alarm or to injure. He was convicted. Allowing his appeal, the Court of Appeal held that there was no unlawful assault without the *mens rea* for assault. Although D might have been guilty on the basis of gross negligence, the judge had misdirected the jury as to what amounted to an unlawful act. The conviction was quashed.

Dangerous unlawful act

For a conviction of constructive manslaughter, the unlawful act must have been dangerous, i.e. such that "all sober and reasonable people would inevitably recognise must subject the other person to, at least, the risk of some harm resulting therefrom, albeit not serious harm", *Church* (1966). By harm, is meant, physical harm. Shock, distress or emotion will not suffice.

Authority: *D.P.P. v Newbury* (1977). The two Ds pushed a paving stone over the side of a bridge as a train approached underneath. It crashed through the window of the cab killing the guard. Convicted of manslaughter the two appealed on the ground that they had not foreseen any harm as a likely result of their actions. Dismissing their appeal, the House of Lords followed the ruling in *Church* and held that where the killing was the result of an unlawful act, the accused was guilty of manslaughter if the act was objectively dangerous. The test was not one of whether the accused recognised the act to be dangerous but whether sober and reasonable people would have recognised the risk of injury to someone. (The report does not mention what the unlawful act was in this case. Since the Ds apparently did not have the *mens rea* for assault, the unlawful act must presumably have been criminal damage, contrary to the Criminal Damage Act 1971, s.1(1).)

Authority: *Dawson* (1985). D and others attempted to rob a filling station, wearing masks and carrying a pickaxe handle and an imitation firearm. The 60-year-old attendant pressed the alarm and the attackers fled. The attendant had a severe heart condition and shortly afterwards died of a heart attack. The Court of Appeal quashed D's manslaughter conviction, holding that the test of whether the act was dangerous was an objective one depending on whether a reasonable person would have recognised the risk of some physical harm to the attendant and the reasonable person must be assumed to know only the facts and circumstances as observed by the defendant. The reasonable person would not have known that the attendant had a weak heart. (In another case, it has been held that if the victim's frailty and old age would have been obvious to a reasonable observer, then at that point the unlawful act may become one which a sober and reasonable person would recognise as carrying the risk of some physical harm, *Watson* (1989)).

Authority: *Cato* (1976). Two drug addicts were unlawfully in possession of heroin. Each prepared for himself a syringe loaded to his own taste with which he then got his friend to inject him. One of them died as a result. The survivor, D, was convicted of two offences: (1) unlawfully and maliciously administering a noxious substance, contrary to the Offences Against the Person Act 1861, s.23; (2) manslaughter. His appeal was dismissed. He had committed an unlawful act (administering a noxious substance) which was dangerous and caused the death. If, instead of D injecting V, V injects himself and dies from the drug, the result will normally be very different, see *Kennedy* (below).

Authority: *Dalby* (1982). D was lawfully in possession of drugs but unlawfully supplied some of them to the deceased who took them himself in a dangerous quantity. The Court of Appeal quashed D's conviction, holding that D's act had not been aimed at the victim. By this, the Court of Appeal meant that D's unlawful act of supply had not caused the death. See *Goodfellow* and *Kennedy* below.

Unlawful act must have caused the death

The unlawful act must have caused the death. It does not, however, have to have been specifically aimed at the victim.

Authority: *Goodfellow* (1986). D set fire to the council house in which he lived. He tried to make it look like a fire bomb in order to persuade the council to rehouse him and his family on the basis that he was homeless. His wife and another were killed in the fire. He appealed against his conviction for manslaughter on the basis that he had aimed his act at the council and had not aimed it at the victims. Dismissing his appeal, the Court of Appeal held that the unlawful act does not have to be aimed at anyone. It simply has to have caused the death. The court dismissed the statement in *Dalby* that the act had to be aimed at the victim, saying that the relevant point in *Dalby* was that the chain of causation must not be broken.

Use of illegal drugs can lead to death. Where D injects V with the illegal drug and V dies of the injection, D is normally guilty of constructive manslaughter since the injecting of the drugs is an unlawful act (administering a noxious substance and/or supplying a controlled drug), is dangerous and has led to the death—see, for example, *Cato* above. Where D supplies the illegal drug to V and it is V who subsequently injects himself or takes the drug orally and then dies of the drug, it will for two reasons be difficult to convict D of constructive manslaughter. First, the supply of the drug, though an unlawful (and presumably dangerous) act, cannot easily be shown to have been a cause of V's death. V's independent decision to take the drug will normally break the chain of causation: *Kennedy* (below). Secondly, D cannot be said to have been a party to an unlawful act by V, since self-injection or consumption of a controlled drug is not an unlawful act: *Dias* (2002).

Authority: *Kennedy* (2007). D prepared a syringe of heroin ready for immediate use and handed it to V. V injected himself and died as a result. The House of Lords quashed D's conviction for manslaughter. The Court of Appeal had certified a question asking "When is it appropriate to find someone guilty of manslaughter where that person has been involved in the supply of a class A controlled drug, which is then freely and voluntarily self-administered by the person to whom it was supplied, and the administration of the drug then causes his death?" The answer from the House of Lords was "In the case of a fully-informed and responsible adult, never". The decision by V to take the drug breaks the chain of causation. [In *Rogers* (2003) D's conviction had been wrongly upheld by the Court of Appeal. In *Rogers*, D had applied and held a tourniquet around the arm of V, a drug abuser, raising a vein into which V had inserted a syringe and injected himself with heroin. Though D may have facilitated or contributed to the administration of the drug by V, he had not administered it. V had injected himself as a result of his own voluntary and informed decision to do so. That broke the chain of causation.]

Manslaughter by gross negligence

The requirements for manslaughter by gross negligence are:

(i) the existence of a duty owed by the accused to the deceased,
(ii) breach of that duty causing death,
(iii) gross negligence.

For the negligence to amount to "gross negligence", it must be something which goes beyond the ordinary civil law concept of negligence, to be such that it warrants criminal liability. It is for the jury to decide whether, having regard to risk of death involved, the accused's act (or omission) was so bad in all the circumstances as to be criminal.

Authority: *Bateman* (1925). D, a doctor, was charged with manslaughter arising out of the death of a patient whose confinement he attended whilst she was giving birth. It was alleged that he was guilty of two aspects of medical negligence and that he had delayed too long in having the patient removed to hospital. He was convicted. He appealed successfully to the Court of Criminal Appeal. It was held that the determining factor in manslaughter was the degree of negligence. It had to be more than merely absence of that ordinary care which in the circumstances a prudent person ought to have taken. It has to have been such that it went beyond a mere matter of compensation between subjects and must have shown such disregard for the life and safety of others as to amount to a crime against the state and be deserving of punishment.

Authority: *Adomako* (1994). D was the anaesthetist at an eye operation. During the operation the tube from the ventilator supplying oxygen to the patient became disconnected. D failed to notice this for a period of six minutes before the patient suffered a cardiac arrest from which the patient died. At D's trial for manslaughter, the judge directed the jury that they could convict if they were satisfied that D was guilty of gross negligence. Dismissing D's appeal against conviction, the House of Lords followed the decision in *Bateman* and held that the test for manslaughter was gross negligence. Their Lordships over-ruled their own decision in *Seymour* (1983) where it had been held that the test of liability was one based on the *Caldwell* definition of recklessness. They made it clear that *Caldwell* recklessness is no part of the test, which is one of gross negligence. Their Lordships made it clear that there is no separate offence of "motor manslaughter". If the killing was by means of a vehicle, then, just as where the killing was caused by any other means, the test of liability for manslaughter was one of gross negligence, as stated in *Andrews v D.P.P.* above.

Authority: *R. v Misra, R. v Srivastava* (2004). After a surgical operation the patient became infected. The two Ds, senior house doctors responsible for the patient's post-operative care, failed to make an adequate diagnosis of the patient's condition, a severe infection requiring aggressive therapy and antibiotics. As a result he died. They were convicted of man-slaughter by gross negligence. Dismissing their appeal, the Court of Appeal held that the definition of the crime is not incompatible with the European Convention on Human Rights, Art.7, entitled "No Punishment without Law" which requires the law to be certain. The ingredients of the offence were clearly defined by the House of Lords in *Adomako* and involve no uncertainty which offends against Art.7. The ingredients are: (i) a negligent breach of a duty of care owed by the defendant to the victim, thereby exposing the victim to the risk of death; (ii) the circumstances were so reprehensible as to amount to gross negligence; (iii) the breach of duty was a substantial cause of the victim's death. There is no additional requirement for the jury to decide whether the defendant's behaviour was a crime. The issue for the jury is not whether the defendant's negligence was gross and whether additionally it is a crime, but whether his behaviour was grossly negligent and consequently criminal.

Manslaughter by omission

For a conviction for manslaughter by omission, the prosecution must (*Khan and Khan*, 1998) prove:

    (a) all the requirements to establish either constructive man-slaughter or manslaughter by gross negligence, and

(b) that the omission which caused death amounted to a breach of a duty owed by the defendant.

For cases where a duty of care has been held to be owed, see pp.7–10 above.

Reckless manslaughter

It is perfectly permissible for a judge to use the word "reckless"—in the ordinary connotation of that term—in describing to the jury the amount of negligence required before it can be found to be "gross": *per* Lord Mackay in *Adomako*. This does not alter the fact that the test for manslaughter by gross negligence is entirely objective, not requiring proof that the defendant himself foresaw any risk of death or injury. There is, however, authority for the existence of a separate category of manslaughter—reckless manslaughter—where the defendant is proved to have carried on his actions, being aware that they involved a high probability of death or serious injury to the deceased: *Lidar* (2000).

4. KILLING A CHILD OR VULNERABLE ADULT

The Domestic Violence, Crime and Victims Act 2004, s.5, created the offence of causing or allowing the death of a child (someone aged under 16) or a vulnerable adult (someone over 16 "whose ability to protect himself from violence, abuse or neglect is significantly impaired through physical or mental disability or illness, through old age or otherwise")—maximum punishment 14 years imprisonment. The requirements for the offence are:

- The victim (V) died as a result of an unlawful act by a person (whether D or someone else), living in the same household as, and having frequent contact with, V.
- The defendant (D) was such a person.
- At the time of the unlawful act, there was a significant risk of physical harm being caused to V by such a person.

Where the victim (e.g. a child or a senile person) lived in a household with two or more others and has clearly been killed by the unlawful act of one of them, the prosecution may well find itself unable to secure a conviction for manslaughter against any member of the household because it is unable to prove which of them committed the fatal unlawful act. For the present offence, however, the prosecution need only prove against each defendant that the fatal unlawful act was committed either by the defendant or by another member of the household. The prosecution does not have to prove which of these two alternatives was the case. However, if it cannot prove that the defendant (D) committed the fatal act, the prosecution must also prove that:

- D was, or ought to have been, aware of the above risk of serious physical harm being caused to V;
- D failed to such steps as he could reasonably have been expected to take to protect V from the risk, and
- the fatal unlawful act occurred in circumstances of the kind that D foresaw, or ought to have foreseen.

5. CORPORATE MANSLAUGHTER

The Corporate Manslaughter and Corporate Homicide Act 2007 creates the offence of corporate manslaughter. Section 1(1) provides:

> 1(1). An organisation to which this section applies is guilty of an offence if the way in which its activities are managed or organised—
> (a) causes a person's death, and
> (b) amounts to a gross breach of a relevant duty of care owed by the organisation to the deceased.

This enactment may make it easier to secure convictions for manslaughter against corporations where corporate failings have led to deaths, e.g. on oil rigs, in rail crashes, in prison cells etc. The organisations which can commit this offence include companies, government departments, police forces and (provided that they are employers) partnerships, trade unions and employers associations. The offence is not committed, however, unless "the way in which the organisation's activities are managed by its senior management is a substantial element" in the gross breach of duty: s.1(3). Thus it is necessary to show failings at a senior level in the organisation, though not necessarily at board level. A gross breach of duty of care amounts to much the same thing as does gross negligence in manslaughter at common law. The relevant duties of care include all of the following: duties owed to the organisation's employees and workers, duties owed as occupier and duties owed in connection with any of the following: the supply by the organisation of goods, services, construction and maintenance work, the carrying on by the organisation of any activity on a commercial basis, the use or keeping by the organisation of plant and machinery. Also included are duties owed to those in custody in police stations, prisons and other custodial institutions.

Secondary liability is expressly excluded. Thus no individual can be charged with aiding, abetting, counselling or procuring the offence of corporate manslaughter. In relation to corporations, the statutory offence of corporate manslaughter replaces the common law offence of manslaughter by gross negligence. Thus organisations which can commit the statutory offence can no longer be guilty of the common law offence of manslaughter by gross negligence, though they could still commit the common law offence of manslaughter by an unlawful act.

6. CAUSING DEATH BY DRIVING

Prompted by the apparent reluctance of juries to convict motorists of manslaughter, Parliament long ago enacted an additional offence, now in the Road Traffic Act 1988, s.1, of causing death by dangerous driving (maximum sentence 14 years imprisonment). In 1991 s.3A was inserted into the Road Traffic Act 1988 creating the offence of causing death by *careless or inconsiderate driving whilst unfit* through drink or drugs or below the drink/drive alcohol limit (maximum sentence 14 years). Now the Road Safety Act 2006 has inserted a new s.2B into the Road Traffic Act 1998 creating a further offence of causing death by *careless or inconsiderate* driving (maximum sentence five years).

Reforms

In its report *Murder, Manslaughter and Infanticide*, Law Com 304 (2006), the Law Commission recommended replacing the current offences of murder and manslaughter with the following graduated series of offences:

1st degree murder (mandatory life sentence)

(a) Killing intentionally, or
(b) Killing where there is an intention to do serious injury coupled with an awareness of a serious risk of causing death.

2nd degree murder (discretionary sentence up to a maximum of life imprisonment)

(a) Killing with an intention to cause serious injury, or
(b) Killing where there is an intention to cause some injury or a fear or risk of injury, coupled with an awareness of a serious risk of causing death, or
(c) Killing reduced from first degree murder by a partial defence (provocation, diminished responsibility or participation in a suicide pact).

Manslaughter (discretionary sentence up to a maximum of life imprisonment)

(a) Killing through gross negligence as to a risk of causing death, or
(b) Killing through a criminal act with either,
　(i) an intention to cause injury or,
　(ii) an awareness of a risk of causing injury, or
(c) Participating in a joint criminal venture in the course of which another participant commits first or second degree murder, in circumstances where the risk of that happening should have been obvious.

The same report recommended allowing *duress* as a defence to first degree and second degree murder and to attempted murder, but subject to two significant qualifications:

(a) the threat must be one of death or life threatening harm, and
(b) the legal burden of proof should be placed on the defendant.

The same report recommended minor amendments to the definition of *diminished responsibility* and also reiterated proposals (in Report 290 on *Partial Defences to Murder* 2004) for amending the definition of *provocation*.

The partial defence of provocation should be reformulated to widen its application to include the use of excessive force in self-defence.

Under the revised formulation of provocation, the defence would apply where:

(a) the defendant acted in response to:
   (i) gross provocation, or
   (ii) fear of serious violence towards himself or another, or
   (iii) a combination of (i) and (ii)
   and
(b) a person of the defendant's age and of ordinary temperament, i.e. ordinary tolerance and self-restraint, in the circumstances of the defendant might have reacted in the same or a similar way. (This would more or less confirm the decision in *Holley* (2005)).

9. THEFT AND RELATED OFFENCES

Theft and the main offences related to it are set out in the Theft Acts 1968 and 1978. This chapter will cover the following: theft, handling, robbery, burglary, blackmail, criminal damage and computer crime.

1. THEFT

Section 1(1) of the 1968 Act states the offence:

> "A person is guilty of theft if he dishonestly appropriates property belonging to another with the intention of permanently depriving the other of it."

Sections 2–6 provide explanations and definitions of elements of s.1 theft, but do not form separate offences.

Actus reus

The *actus reus* of theft consists of the act of appropriation of property and the circumstance that the property belongs to another.

Appropriation

Section 3(1) of the 1968 Act states:

> "Any assumption by a person of the rights of an owner amounts to an appropriation . . .".

Although the commonest form of assumption may be taking property away, destroying property, treating property as one's own and selling it are also covered. Also under s.3(1), a later assumption of a right, e.g. by keeping property after it should be returned, can amount to an appropriation.

Two House of Lords' decisions, *Lawrence* (1971) and *Morris* (1984) gave conflicting interpretations of appropriation. The issue was whether an act which is done with consent, i.e. an act authorised by the owner, can amount to an appropriation. An example is where D, using a worthless cheque has bought goods from his victim. Is it theft when D takes the goods, which the victim voluntarily hands over? The House of Lords in *Gomez* held that the ruling in *Lawrence* was the correct one and that consent is no defence to theft. Although the decision itself in *Morris* was correct, some parts of the speeches were incorrect. Thus an act can be an appropriation notwithstanding that it was authorised or done with the consent of the owner. It is not necessary for there to be an adverse interference with, or usurpation of, some right of the owner. For there to be an appropriation, it is sufficient if there is an assumption of one, or more, rights of the owner. Of course, an appropriation will not itself amount to theft unless accompanied by dishonesty and the other ingredients of the offence.

Authority: *Morris* (1984), *Anderson v Burnside* (1984). The behaviour of the two Ds was similar. In *Morris* D took items from supermarket shelves and replaced the correct labels with ones showing lower prices. He took the items to the checkout and paid the lower price. In *Anderton v Burnside* D took the label off a joint of meat and placed it on a more expensive joint. His act was discovered before he got to the checkout. The House of Lords upheld the convictions in both cases and held that as the offence is committed at the moment of appropriation it was irrelevant that D in *Anderton v Burnside* had not left the shop.

Authority: *Gomez* (1992). D dishonestly persuaded his employer to accept what D knew to be a worthless cheque in payment for some electrical goods. Thus his employer consented to D handing over the goods to the fraudster presenting the cheque. D was convicted of theft of the goods, and appealed on the ground that because his supplying of the goods was with the consent of the owner, there could be no appropriation. Their Lordships held that the defendant was guilty of theft, because he had supplied the goods and that was sufficient for an appropriation.

Authority: *Hinks* (2000). D became friendly with a man who was naive, gullible and of limited intelligence. She influenced him to withdraw sums totalling £60,000 from his building society, which D deposited in her own bank account. She was charged with theft of them. Her defence was that they were gifts or at least loans. Convicted, she appealed arguing that there cannot be an appropriation and therefore cannot be a theft if there is valid gift or a valid transfer of ownership to the defendant. The House of Lords rejected that argument as inconsistent with the decisions in *Lawrence* and *Gomez* and dismissed her appeal. [After *Gomez* and *Hinks*, it is clear that consent is irrelevant to the issue of appropriation—though it may be relevant to the issue of dishonesty. In *Hinks* the majority of the House of Lords clearly considered D to be dishonest and thus found it unnecessary in that particular case to pronounce upon what directions on dishonesty should be given in such cases. See *Wheatley*, p.129 below.]

The duration of theft can be important for a number of reasons, including:

(i) the offence of handling stolen property can be committed only "otherwise than in the course of the stealing";
(ii) if the theft is finished before any force is used or threatened, there can be no robbery, since for robbery the theft must be accompanied, or immediately preceded, by the use or threat of force;
(iii) goods which have once been stolen cannot be stolen again by the same thief exercising the same, or other rights, of ownership over them.

Authority: *Atakpu* (1994). D and a colleague hired cars in Germany on false documents, intending to bring them to England to sell them. They were arrested at Dover and charged with conspiracy to steal. They were only liable if what they had agreed, if carried out, would be an offence triable in England or Wales. If carried out abroad, it would not be so triable. The Court of Appeal held that they could not be liable. The theft had clearly been completed in Germany and D could not be said to be stealing them when days later he brought them to England to dispose of.

Property

Property is defined by s.4 to include real and personal property, money and intangible property, such as credit in a bank account. There are some exceptions under s.4.

To cause a reduction in the size of V's bank account is to appropriate intangible property belonging to V (namely V's right to sue the bank for the amount by which the account is reduced).

Authority: *Williams (Roy)* (2000). D, a builder, dishonestly over-billed for work which he had done. In payment, D received from V a cheque which he paid into his account. This was a genuine cheque but obtained dishonestly. By paying it into his account, D dishonestly appropriated part of the credit in V's bank account. D was thus guilty of the theft of that amount of the credit in V's bank account. [The result would have been the same if D had forged the cheque: *Burke* (2000).]

Authority: *Hilton* (1997). D, the chairman of a charitable organisation, dishonestly caused the organisation's bank to transfer sums of money, on two occasions, by sending instructions by fax and on another by writing a cheque. He was convicted of theft of intangible property, namely some of the organisation's credit balance in its bank account. The Court of Appeal held that he was still guilty even if the bank was bound, as debtor of the organisation (its customer), to replenish the account. (There will be no theft, however, unless, at the time of the dishonest withdrawal, either the account was in credit or else the debit balance was within an authorised overdraft limit, *Kohn* (1979), *Forsyth* (1997). If the facts of *Hilton, Williams (Roy)* or *Burke* occurred again today, the appropriate charge would be fraud contrary to s.1 of the Fraud Act 2006—see Ch.10 below.)

Authority: *Briggs* (2003). Mr & Mrs B agreed to buy a house. By deception, D persuaded them to authorise the transfer of some of their money to the vendor's solicitor. D deceived them into thinking the house would be conveyed into their names. In fact it was conveyed into the names of D and D's father. D was guilty of a deception offence but was held not to be guilty of theft. Where a victim causes a payment to be made in reliance on deceptive conduct by D, there is no appropriation by D. *Hilton* was distinguished since in *Hilton* the defendant had committed physical acts amounting to an appropriation (sending a fax and writing a cheque causing the debits from the victim's bank account).

By virtue of s.4(3):

(i) Land cannot generally be stolen.
(ii) Picking wild plants unless done for sale, reward or other commercial gain will not be theft.
(iii) A wild animal cannot be stolen unless it has been, or is in the process of being, reduced into possession of another person.

Information is not property and information dishonestly obtained has presented difficulties. This is now covered by the Computer Misuse Act 1990 (see below).

Electricity is not property, but there is a separate offence (in s.13) of dishonestly wasting or diverting electricity.

Neither a human corpse, nor parts of a corpse, are property capable of being stolen. They are, however, property capable of being stolen if they have acquired different attributes by virtue of the application of skill, such as dissection or preservation techniques, for exhibition or teaching purposes, *Kelly* (1998). In *Kelly* the Court of Appeal suggested, obiter, that they might qualify as property, even without the acquisition of different attributes, if they have a use or significance beyond their mere existence, e.g. they are intended for use as an organ transplant or for DNA extraction or even as an exhibit at a trial.

Belonging to another

Under s.5(1), property is regarded as belonging to anyone having possession or control of it or having a proprietary right or interest in it.

Authority: *Shadrokh-Cigari* (1988). D was guardian of a minor. Funds for the minor were transferred from an American to an English bank, but the American bank over-credited the account. D got the minor to sign drafts credited to him, and he had spent most of the excess money before he was discovered. He was convicted of theft, and appealed. His appeal was dismissed. The court held that there were two routes to a conviction. Under s.5(4) (below) he had obtained property by another's mistake, and was therefore liable, but the court also held that because of the mistake the bank retained an equitable interest in the drafts and therefore the situation was still covered by s.5(1). Section 5(4) was not really necessary.

Authority: *Hallam and Blackburn* (1995). Ds were financial advisers who paid cheques from, or meant for, their clients into their own accounts. They were charged with theft of the money at the time they paid them in. The Court of Appeal held that the clients (investors) had retained an equitable interest in the cheques and the proceeds of those cheques. [This was different from the situation where a client of a travel agent pays the agent a cheque for a holiday or flights. In that situation the client does not retain an equitable interest.]

Provided he has the necessary *mens rea*, a person can steal his own property from someone with a lesser interest.

Authority: *Turner* (1971). D had taken his car to a garage to be repaired. When it was repaired he took it from where it was parked, intending not to pay for the repair. The court held that the car "belonged to" the repairer at the time D took it as the repairer had control over it. D was therefore guilty of theft. There are some circumstances where legal ownership, possession and control have all passed to the defendant but for the purposes of the Theft Act the property is treated as still belonging to the original owner. Section 5(3) states:

> "Where a person receives property from or on account of another, and is under an obligation to the other to retain and deal with that property or its proceeds in a particular way, the property or proceeds shall be regarded (as against him) as belonging to the other."

This subsection is relevant only where ownership of the goods has passed, and is therefore mainly concerned with money given to a person to deal with in a particular way.

Authority: *Davidge v Bunnett* (1984). D's flatmates gave D money to pay certain household bills. D spent the proceeds on Christmas presents. D was guilty of theft. D was under a legal obligation to use the money in a particular way and therefore the money was property belonging to another by virtue of s.5(3).

Authority: *Hall* (1973). D was a travel agent who had taken money for holidays and not booked them. His business collapsed and the money was lost. Although D had a general obligation to fulfil his contract he did not have to deal with those specific notes and cheques in a particular way. He did not have to keep a separate account with the money in. Thus s.5(3) did not apply.

Where people contract on the basis that their money will be safeguarded by trusteeship, there is a legal obligation within the meaning of s.5(3).

Authority: *Klineberg and Marsden* (1998). Purchasers of timeshares had paid the price to D on terms that D would pay the money to a stakeholder who would release it to the seller when the timeshare properties were ready for occupation or else would refund it to the purchasers. The money never reached the stakeholder. D was held to have committed theft of the purchase price or its proceeds; D had been obliged to deal with the price in a certain way, which by s.5(3) was thus to be regarded as belonging to the purchasers.

Authority: *Wain* (1997). D had raised almost £3,000 for a "Telethon". He opened a separate bank account under the name "Scarborough Telethon appeal" and deposited the money in that account. He withdrew money from the account for himself and was convicted of theft. His appeal failed, the Court of Appeal holding that he had been under an obligation to deal with the proceeds of the sums collected (if not the actual notes and coins) by keeping in existence a fund sufficient to pay the money. Thus by s.5(3) the money was property belonging to another.

Section 5(4) provides:

> "Where a person gets property by another's mistake, and is under an obligation to make restoration (in whole or in part) of the property or its proceeds or of the value thereof, then to the extent of that obligation the property or proceeds shall be regarded (as against him) as belonging to the person entitled to restoration . . .".

Section 5(4) applies where the possession, control and ownership have all passed to the defendant, but where the defendant got the property by a mistake and is under a duty to restore it or its value. In this situation the property is still regarded as belonging to another.

Authority: *Attorney-General's Reference No.1 of 1983*. D was mistakenly paid an extra £74 in wages for work she had not done. When she found out she did nothing. It was held that s.5(4) applied because she was under an obligation to make restoration of the money. Thus, assuming that she dishonestly decided not to repay it, she was guilty of theft.

The obligation to repay must be a legal one and not merely a moral one, *Gilks* (1972).

Mens rea of theft

There are two elements of *mens rea* in theft: dishonesty and intention to deprive permanently.

Dishonesty

Dishonesty is partially defined in s.2(1) of the 1968 Act, which sets out three situations where as a matter of law a person is *not* dishonest:

(a) Where he believes he has in law the right to deprive the other of the property.
(b) Where he believes that the other person would have consented to the appropriation if he had known of the appropriation and the circumstances of it: for example unauthorisedly "borrowing" consumable goods from a neighbour or money from a friend's purse.
(c) (Unless he is a trustee or personal representative), where he acts in the belief that the true owner cannot be found by taking reasonable steps.

Section 2(2) states that a person can be found to be dishonest notwithstanding his willingness to pay for the property. If an owner does not want to sell then it can be dishonest to act against his will and take the property and leave payment.

In situations not covered by s.2(1), the meaning of dishonesty, as an ordinary word in the English language, is for the jury to decide.

Authority: *Feely* (1973). D, a shop manager, took £30 from the shop till. He said he had intended to repay it. The judge directed the jury that D was dishonest in these circumstances but the Court of Appeal held that dishonesty was a question of fact for the jury to decide according to the standards of the ordinary decent person.

This test became further refined in *Ghosh* (1982) where the Court of Appeal set out a two-stage test for dishonesty:

(i) The jury must decide if D's behaviour was dishonest by the standards of the ordinary decent person. If it was not, he is not guilty.
(ii) If his behaviour was dishonest by those ordinary decent standards D is nevertheless not dishonest unless he *realised* that people would so regard his behaviour.

Thus D is dishonest if he knows that, by the ordinary standards of society, people would regard him as dishonest.

Authority: *Wheatley and another v Commissioner of Police of the British Virgin Islands* (2006). D had authority to make contracts on behalf of the government (his employer) to buy goods and services up to the value of $60,000 and to authorise payments under those contracts. He was required, however, to get specific clearance to deal with any supplier in which he had an interest. He made contracts with two suppliers to re-erect a wall, the work being shared and the price of each contract being conveniently just under $60,000. The work was done and payments, authorised by D, were made to the two contractors. D had a financial interest in both suppliers and at no stage disclosed this to his employer. Nevertheless, the work had been done and the government had not been overcharged or suffered any loss. D was charged with theft of the money paid to the suppliers. He argued that there could be no dishonesty where the contract had been made and services rendered for an appropriate price. The Privy Council rejected that argument, holding that there was ample evidence of D's dishonesty and the offence of theft does not require that a victim is the poorer as a result of it. [After this case, it seems clear that the *Ghosh* test for dishonesty applies in all cases other than the three situations in which s.2(1) states that there is no dishonesty. Lord Hutton's dissenting opinion in *Hinks*, that there can be no dishonesty where D accepts a valid gift, is not the law.]

Intention permanently to deprive

A conditional intention to deprive the owner permanently is not sufficient.

Authority: *Easom* (1971). D sat in a cinema, helped himself to the handbag of a woman sitting nearby, looked into it, found nothing of interest and replaced the bag with all of its contents. It was held that a conditional intention, i.e. an intention to steal if he found something of value, was not enough to convict him of theft. (If properly charged, he could on those facts be convicted of attempted theft—see attempting the impossible, p.51 above).

Section 6(1) provides:

> "A person appropriating property belonging to another without meaning the other permanently to lose the thing itself is nevertheless to be regarded as having the intention of permanently depriving the other of it if his intention is to treat the thing as his own to dispose of regardless of the other's rights; and a borrowing or lending of it may amount to so treating it if . . . the borrowing or lending is for a period and in circumstances amounting to an outright taking or disposal".

It used to be thought that this subsection would apply only when the thing returned was completely used up, e.g. a season ticket that had expired or a battery which was completely flat. It is now clear that it may apply to a person in possession or control of another's property who, dishonestly and for his own purpose, deals with that property in such a manner that he knows he is *risking* its loss, *Fernandez* (1996).

Authority: *Marshall, Coombes and Eren* (1998). The three Ds were video recorded obtaining underground tickets or travel cards from members of the public passing through the barriers and re-selling them to other potential customers. The tickets stated on the reverse that they remained the property of London Underground. Convicted of theft of the tickets, the Ds appealed claiming they had not intended to deprive the owner (London Underground) permanently since the tickets would in each case find their way back to London Underground when used by the purchasers. Dismissing their appeals, the Court of Appeal held that s.6(1) applied. By acquiring and re-selling the tickets the Ds were treating them as their own to dispose regardless of the rights of the owner.

2. HANDLING

Section 22 of the 1968 Act provides that a person is guilty of handling stolen goods if, knowing or believing them to be stolen, and acting other than in the course of stealing, he dishonestly does one of the following:

   (i) Receives the goods.
  (ii) Arranges to receive them.
 (iii) Undertakes their detention, removal, disposal or realisation by or for the benefit of another.
 (iv) Arranges to undertake the above.
  (v) Assists in their detention, removal, disposal or realisation, etc.
 (vi) Arranges to assist in the above.

Except where the form of the offence is receiving (or arranging to receive) the goods, the offence is committed only if the defendant acted "for the benefit of another".

Actus reus of handling

"Stolen goods"

The various different ways, just listed, in which the offence can be committed all require that the goods are "stolen" goods at the time the handling offence is alleged to have been committed. Thus, if the defendant is alleged to have committed the offence by "arranging" to receive or "arranging" to assist, then the goods must already have been stolen at the time the arranging was done.

>   (i) Section 24(4) states that goods are "stolen goods" if they were obtained by theft, or blackmail or by being obtained by fraud contrary to s.1 of the Fraud Act 2006.
> (ii) They cease to be "stolen goods", after they have been restored to the person from whom they were stolen or to other lawful possession or custody (e.g. that of the police), section 24(3).
> (iii) They also cease to be "stolen goods" after the person from whom they were stolen ceases to have a right to restitution of them.
> (iv) "Stolen goods" include any other goods which directly or indirectly represent them as being the proceeds of their realisation or disposal, s.24(2).

Authority: *Park* (1987). D arranged to handle cheques which were to be paid into his account, but at the time of the arrangement, the cheques had not been stolen. The Court of Appeal quashed his conviction for handling, because for the offence to be committed the goods must be stolen at the time the arrangement is made.

Authority: *Attorney-General's Reference No.1 of 1974.* A constable saw an unlocked unattended car containing goods which he suspected (correctly) had been stolen. He removed the rotor arm from the car to immobilise it and waited nearby. Ten minutes later D appeared and tried to start the car. The constable then questioned and arrested him. D was acquitted of handling stolen goods. The Court of Appeal stated that the goods were to be regarded as returned to lawful possession (i.e. that of the constable) only if he had assumed control over them—and that depended upon his intention. If his only object in immobilising the car was to ensure that the driver could not drive off without first being questioned, then the goods were not reduced into his possession or control. The issue of the constable's intention should have been left for the jury to decide.

"For the benefit of another"

The requirement (other than where the charge is based on receiving or arranging to receive) that the defendant acted "for the benefit of another" distinguishes thieves who are merely disposing of the goods they have stolen from those properly to be regarded as handlers of stolen property. Thus, the thief who sells to an innocent third person the property he has stolen is not guilty of handling. He cannot be said to be acting by or for the benefit of the innocent purchaser, but simply for his own benefit, *Bloxham* (1983). On the other hand, a defendant who knows that the goods are stolen and obliges someone else by keeping them in his house, will be guilty of handling by assisting in their retention for the benefit of another, *Brown* (1969). If initially the defendant does not know they are stolen but acquires that knowledge later, then if he continues to keep them in his house, he will then become guilty of handling, *Pitchley* (1973).

Authority: *Kanwar* (1982). D lied to police to protect her husband who had brought stolen goods into the house. She lied saying that they were in fact hers. It was held in the Court of Appeal that she was guilty of handling by assisting in their retention for the benefit of her husband.

"Otherwise than in the course of the stealing"

It is a question of fact as to whether the stealing has been completed. If it has not, the continuation of the stealing cannot be handling. For other reasons why it may matter whether the theft has been completed, see "Appropriation" and *Atakpu* (p.124 above) and *Hale* (p.135 below).

Authority: *Pitham and Hehl* (1976). M knew that a certain householder, X, was in prison. M went to the X's house with P and H to sell them some of X's furniture. P and H appealed against their convictions for handling (by receiving) claiming that their handling was "in the course of the stealing" (i.e. by M). The Court of Appeal dismissed their appeals, holding that M had appropriated the furniture by inviting P and H to the house and inviting them to buy it. Thus the appropriation (i.e. the stealing) was complete before P and H "received" it.

Mens rea of handling

The defendant has to have acted dishonestly and with knowledge or belief that the goods are stolen. For the meaning of "dishonestly", see *Ghosh* (p.129 above). As to knowledge or belief:

  (i) the question of knowledge or belief is a subjective one, *Atwal v Massey* (1971);
 (ii) mere suspicion does not amount to knowledge or belief, *Grainge* (1974);
(iii) buying goods realising they may be stolen and taking a chance does not amount to knowledge or belief, *Ismail* (1977);
 (iv) a direction which includes references to "wilful blindness" or "closing one's eyes" or that the defendant should have been "put on inquiry" is faulty unless it is made clear that these expressions do not detract from the requirement of knowledge or belief, *Ismail* (1977), *Belenie* (1980); such expressions are better omitted from the direction.
  (v) according to *Hall* (1995), knowledge and belief are different things; D has knowledge if he was told by someone, such as the thief, with first hand knowledge; D may believe where he has not been told on such direct authority but nevertheless knows there is no explanation other than that the goods are stolen. Still, however, mere suspicion is insufficient.

3. RETENTION OF A WRONGFUL CREDIT

Section 24A was inserted into the Theft Act 1968 by the Theft (Amendment) Act 1996. By it, someone whose account is wrongfully credited is guilty of an offence if he knows or believes that the credit is wrongful and dishonestly fails to take reasonable steps to secure that the credit is cancelled. A credit is "wrongful" if it derives from any of theft, blackmail, stolen goods or fraud contrary of the Fraud Act 2006, s.1. This offence is akin to handling except that here the criminal is not handling goods but has received the proceeds of crime credited into his bank account.

4. OTHER OFFENCES UNDER THE 1968 ACT

The following offences, covered by the 1968 Act, are dealt with to some extent in most syllabuses. However, they tend to be covered only briefly, as they are here, being relatively straightforward and presenting few problems.

Robbery

Under s.8(1) of the 1968 Act:

> "A person is guilty of robbery if he steals, and immediately before or at the time of doing so and in order to do so, he uses force on any person or puts or seeks to put any person in fear of being then and there subject to force."

Force or fear of force

Robbery is an aggravated form of theft. What turns theft into robbery is the use of force, or putting or seeking to put someone in fear of force. The force must be against the person and not against property. The force or threat must be used in order to steal.

Immediately before or at the time of stealing

If force is not used or threatened until after the theft is finished, then robbery is not committed. When the theft is completed is a question of fact for the jury to decide given all the circumstances.

Authority: *Hale* (1979). One D carried out the appropriation while the other tied up the victim in another room. The court held that theft was a continuing offence and could have continued while the goods were being removed from the premises, which is when the force took place. It was up to the jury to decide on the facts.

Authority: *Lockley* (1995). D and others took beer from an off licence and when approached by the shop keeper, used violence towards him. They argued, using *Gomez*, that the theft was complete before violence was used. Dismissing their appeal against convictions for robbery, the Court of Appeal held that *Hale* still applied and it was up to the jury to decide whether the theft was still continuing. (For other decisions on the duration of theft see *Atakpu* (p.124 above) and *Pitham and Hehl* (p.133 above).)

Burglary

Under s.9(1) of the 1968 Act burglary can be committed in two ways:

(a) By entering any building or part of a building as a trespasser and with intent to commit theft, grievous bodily harm or criminal damage (s.9(1)(a));
(b) Having entered the premises as a trespasser, by stealing or attempting to steal, or inflicting or attempting to inflict grievous bodily harm (s.9(1)(b)).

Mens rea

For s.9(1)(a) the defendant must at the time of entry have the intention to commit the further offence—though it is immaterial whether he does in fact later go on to commit that further offence. For s.9(1)(b) the defendant does not have to have any further intent when he enters, though here he does not commit burglary unless having entered, he actually does then go on to commit, or at least to attempt, one of the two offences listed. For both (a) and (b) it is necessary that at the time of entry, the defendant has a further element of *mens rea*. This is that at the time of entry he knows, or is reckless (in a *Cunningham* sense) as to, the fact that he is entering as a trespasser.

Authority: *Collins* (1973). Stripped naked of everything except his socks, D climbed up the outside of a house to the window sill of the bedroom of an 18-year-old girl. There he saw her apparently welcome him in. He entered through the window and had sexual intercourse with the girl. Only afterwards did she realise that D was not her boyfriend. His conviction for burglary (with intent to rape) was quashed because the Court of Appeal could not be sure that at the time of D's entry, (i.e. through the window) he knew, or was reckless as to, the fact that he was entering as a trespasser, i.e. unlawfully. [Until 2003, rape was one of the crimes listed in s.9(1)(a). It was removed from the list by the Sexual Offences Act 2003 and replaced by the offence (in s.63 of the 2003 Act) of trespass with intent to commit a sexual offence.]

Actus reus

The *actus reus* requires an entry. In *Collins*, the court said, obiter, that the entry had to be "substantial and effective". In *Brown* (1985), the top half of D's body was inside a broken shop window, his feet still on the ground outside, whilst he apparently was rummaging through goods inside. He was held to be properly convicted of burglary, his entry clearly having been "effective".

Authority: *Ryan* (1996). D was found trapped with his head and right arm inside the window of a house, the rest of his body being outside. His appeal against a conviction for burglary was dismissed. The Court of Appeal held that a person could enter even if only part of his body was actually inside and it was totally irrelevant whether or not he was capable of stealing anything as a result of the entry.

Entry must be into a building or part of a building and must be entry as a trespasser. Broadly, this means entry with neither a legal right of entry nor the permission of the occupier. Entry in excess of permission given will be entry as a trespasser.

Authority: *Jones and Smith* (1976). S had general permission from his father to enter his father's house. S and J both entered the house intending to steal inside. It was held that S as well as J was guilty of burglary. He had entered in excess of the permission given (since clearly that permission did not extend to any entry in order to steal) and he had entered knowing, or at least being recklessness as to, that fact.

Authority: *Walkington* (1979). D entered an Oxford Street store near closing time when cashiers were cashing-up. He went to where a till was unattended at the centre of a three-sided counter and went into that area (which was prohibited to customers) intending to steal from the till (which was in fact empty). He was held guilty of burglary in that he entered that part of the building as a trespasser with intent to steal.

Aggravated burglary

By s.10, aggravated burglary is committed when the burglar has with him at the time a firearm, imitation firearm, offensive weapon or explosive. Imitation firearm would include a toy gun. Anything made, adapted or intended to be used as a weapon is covered by the definition. The section does not require that the defendant has an intention of using the weapon except where the weapon is not a firearm or explosive and is not an "article made or adapted for use for causing injury to or incapacitating a person". In that exceptional case it must be proved that the defendant had an intention to use it to cause injury or to incapacitate. Even then, however, it is enough that his intention is an intention to use it if he has to; and it does not necessarily have to be an intention to use it during the course of the burglary.

Authority: *Stones* (1989). D had with him an ordinary kitchen knife which he intended to use to defend himself if he was attacked by a gang—though not necessarily during burglary. The Court of Appeal held that this was sufficient for liability.

Blackmail

Under s.21(1):

"A person is guilty of blackmail if with a view to gain for himself or another or with intent to cause loss to another, he makes any unwarranted demand with menaces, and for this purpose a demand with menaces is unwarranted unless the person making it does so in the belief—
(a) that he has reasonable grounds for making the demand; *and*
(b) that the use of the menaces is a proper means of reinforcing the demand."

"With a view to gain or intent to cause loss"

Gain and loss are defined only in terms of money or property, although gain includes keeping what one has and loss includes not getting what one otherwise might get (s.34).

"Unwarranted demand"

A demand is made when it is spoken or posted, even if it is not heard or received, *Treacy* (1971). According to the words of s.21(1), the test of whether a demand is unwarranted is a subjective one depending on the belief of the defendant when he makes the demand.

"Menaces"

As an ordinary word in the English language, this is easily understood by a jury. The menaces must be "of such a nature and extent that the mind of an ordinary person of normal stability and courage might be influenced or made apprehensive so as to concede unwillingly to the demand", *Clear* (1968).

Authority: *Harry* (1974). D, a treasurer of a student Rag committee, sent letters to 115 shopkeepers asking them to buy indemnity posters costing between £1 and £5 "to protect you from any Rag Activity. . .". The judge quoted the test laid down in *Clear* as to what is a menace, found that there was no evidence of any such menace and directed the jury to acquit.

5. CRIMINAL DAMAGE

Criminal damage offences are covered by a separate Act of Parliament, the Criminal Damage Act 1971. Under s.1(1) of the 1971 Act:

> "A person who without lawful excuse destroys or damages any property belonging to another intending to destroy or damage any such property or being reckless as to whether any such property would be destroyed or damaged shall be guilty of an offence."

Actus reus

This consists of destroying or damaging property belonging to another. Property is defined as tangible property, including land, and therefore differs from property under the Theft Act. "Belonging to another" however has substantially the same meaning as in the 1968 Act, although there is no equivalent to s.5 of that Act.

The destruction or damage must be more than merely nominal, although not necessarily irreversible.

The following have been held to amount to "damage": writing graffiti on a concrete pillar or wall with a marker pen; spraying paint on to a pavement so that the local authority had to remove it with pressure water jets; applying mud to a ceiling; dumping waste on a building site costing a lot to remove; jumping on a policeman's helmet temporarily preventing it serving its normal function. On the other hand, spitting on a policeman's uniform has been held not to cause damage. The Computer Misuse Act 1990, s.3(6) provides that for the purposes of the Criminal Damage Act 1971, modifying the contents of a computer shall not be regarded as damaging the computer or any computer storage medium unless it impairs its physical condition. This is because such interference is now caught by offences under the 1990 Act.

Mens rea

The necessary *mens rea* for criminal damage is intention or recklessness. The *Caldwell* definition of recklessness is no longer part of the law: *R. v G* (2003)—explained in Ch.2.

Lawful excuse

Under s.5(2) of the Act a defence of lawful excuse is available if:

(a) the defendant honestly thought he had the consent of the relevant person, or would have if that person had known the circumstances or
(b) he acted as he did in order to protect property he thought in immediate need of protection, and he believed the means used were reasonable.

The test of such belief is subjective: provided the belief is honest it does not matter that it was unreasonable. See *Jaggard v Dickinson* (Ch.6). Nevertheless, the subsection is still interpreted strictly.

Authority: *Johnson v D.P.P.* (1994). D was a squatter who replaced locks on the door of his squat and damaged door frames in doing so. Although he believed he had a need of protection, the Divisional Court held that he did not have a defence under s.5(2) because he did not believe his need, or the threat, was imminent and necessitated only that action. The only possibility was a speculative future need of protection, and that was not enough.

Aggravated criminal damage

Under s.1(2) of the 1971 Act it is an offence intentionally or recklessly to destroy or damage property intending to endanger life thereby or being reckless as to whether life is endangered thereby. The maximum punishment is life imprisonment. The property does not have to belong to another. The lawful excuse defence provided by s.5(2) does not apply to aggravated criminal damage, though the defendant is entitled to rely on any general defence available at common law.

It is a *mens rea* requirement that the defendant intended to endanger life, or was reckless as to doing so. That requirement is absent if the defendant did not realise that there was a risk that human life would be endangered. The defendant does not actually have to have endangered human life. The word "thereby" is important. The defendant has to have intended *by the criminal damage or destruction* to endanger life, or else to have been reckless as to whether life would be endangering life *by the criminal damage or destruction*.

Authority: *Steer* (1987). D fired a rifle at the door and windows of a house. No injuries were caused to the people who were in the bungalow. D was charged, inter alia, with damaging property with intent, being reckless as to whether the life of another would be thereby endangered, contrary to s.1(2) of the Criminal Damage Act 1971. The House of Lords held that the judge had been right to decide that there was no case to answer. The intention or recklessness envisaged by s.1(2) of the 1971 Act was directed to the possible danger to life caused by the destroyed or damaged property. It was not sufficient that D intended, or was reckless as to, life being endangered by his act of shooting. To be guilty under s.1(2) he had to intend to endanger life by the criminal damage, (i.e. by means of the broken glass) or be reckless as to endangering life by the criminal damage.

It may be that the defendant causes damage different from that which he intended, or was reckless as to causing. In determining whether the defendant intended to endanger life by the criminal damage (or was reckless as to doing so), one looks not at the criminal damage which he actually caused, but at the criminal damage he intended to cause or was reckless as to causing. Thus, even if the damage actually caused is slight, there can still be liability under s.1(2) if the defendant intended by criminal damage to endanger life or if he was aware of a danger to life from the damage he intended, *Dudley* (1989).

Authority: *R. v Webster, R. v Warwick* (1995). In the first case, D dropped a heavy stone over a railway bridge on to a passing train. It penetrated the roof damaging it and roof material showered down on passengers, none of whom was injured. The Court of Appeal held that D's conviction under s.1(2) could not be justified on the basis that D had intended by his act (of dropping the stone) to endanger life, (i.e. by the stone hitting a passenger), but it could be justified on the basis that he had been reckless as to whether life would be endangered by the damage he was reckless as to causing, (i.e. the damage to the roof causing material to shower down on the passengers.) In the second case, D had driven a car from which bricks were thrown at a police car, smashing its windows and showering the occupants with glass. D had then rammed his car into the police car several times. It was held that liability under s.1(2) did not depend upon whether the car window was broken but on whether D intended to break it and whether he intended or was reckless as to whether any resulting damage would endanger life. The judge had properly directed the jury and the conviction was upheld.

Arson

Under s.1(3), if either of the above offences under s.1(1) and 1(2) is committed by fire the offence is one of arson punishable by a maximum of life imprisonment.

6. COMPUTER MISUSE

The law criminalising computer misuse is contained in the Computer Misuse Act 1990. Under section 1(1) of the Act a person commits an offence if:

(a) he causes a computer to perform any function with intent to secure access to any program or data held in any computer;

(b) the access he intends to secure is unauthorised; and

(c) he knows at the time when he causes the computer to perform the function that this is the case.

This offence is the basic "hacking" offence which does not require actual access or any damage or securing of information. It is a crime of specific intent. It may be committed by D using one computer to access another, or by D gaining access to one computer in order to access data on that same computer: *Attorney-General's Reference No. 1 of 1991* (1992). The offence requires an intent to secure "unauthorised access". This covers all forms of unauthorised access, whether by insiders or outsiders. Where D is authorised to access some data (e.g. a range of accounts at the bank where D works) but not to access other data (e.g. other accounts), accessing the latter will amount to unauthorised access: *R. v Bow Street Magistrates Court, ex parte Government of United States of America* (1999).

Under s.2 of the Act there is an aggravated offence of committing an offence under s.1 with intent to commit or facilitate the commission of a further offence punishable with five years or more.

Section 3 creates a separate offence of unauthorised modification of the contents of a computer in order to impair operation, reliability or access. This is designed mainly to criminalise the introducction of computer viruses.

———————

10. FRAUD AND NON-PAYMENT

The Fraud Act 2006 repealed the deception offences previously to be found in the Theft Acts 1968 and 1978. Many of those former deception offences involved the defendant in obtaining something (property, a pecuniary advantage, services, a money transfer) dishonestly by deception. The Fraud Act replaced them with other offences, the two principal offences being fraud (s.1) and obtaining services dishonestly (s.11).

1. FRAUD

Fraud is an offence contrary to the Fraud Act 2006, s.1. Sections 2, 3 and 4 set out the three different ways in which the offence can be committed: by false representation (s.2); by failing to comply with a legal duty to disclose information (s.3); by abuse of position (s.4). Fraud by false representation will surely be the most common.

Fraud by false representation—section 2

Section 2 provides:

(1) A person is in breach of this section if he:
   (a) dishonestly makes a false representation, and
   (b) intends, by making the false representation—
       (i) to make a gain for himself or another, or
       (ii) to cause loss to another or to expose another to a risk of loss.
(2) A representation is false if—
   (a) it is untrue or misleading, and
   (b) the person making it knows that it is, or might be, untrue or misleading.
(3) "Representation" means any representation as to fact or law, including a representation as to the state of mind of—
   (a) the person making the representation, or
   (b) any other person.
(4) A representation may be express or implied.
(5) For the purposes of this section a representation may be regarded as made if it (or anything implying it) is submitted in any form to any system or device designed to receive, convey or respond to communications (with or without human intervention).

The *actus reus* is making a false representation. The are two required elements of *mens rea*:

(a) dishonesty (the test is that laid down in *Ghosh*, see p.129 above), and
(b) an intention, by making the false representation, to make a gain or to cause a loss (or risk causing a loss) to another person.

"Gain" and "loss" have similar meanings to those relevant for the offence of blackmail (p.138 above). Section 5 of the Fraud Act 2006 states:

(1) The references to gain and loss in sections 2 to 4 are to be read in accordance with this section.
(2) 'Gain' and 'loss'—
 (a) extend only to gain or loss in money or other property;
 (b) include any such gain or loss whether temporary or permanent;
 and 'property' means any property whether real or personal (including things in action and other intangible property).
(3) 'Gain' includes a gain by keeping what one has, as well as a gain by getting by what one does not have.
(4) 'Loss' includes a loss by not getting what one might get, as well as a loss by parting with what one has.

Knowingly putting a foreign coin into a vending machine amounts to fraud by representation: see s.2(5). Also caught is someone who knowingly tells lies when: (i) applying for a job; (ii) applying for insurance; (iii) making an insurance claim; (iv) applying for a mortgage loan or an overdraft; (iv) begging. The offence is committed even if the intended gain (or loss) is never actually achieved, e.g. because the person hearing or reading the lie recognises it for what it is.

Fraud by failing to disclose information—section 3

By s.3 fraud is committed by someone who

(a) dishonestly fails to disclose to another person information which he is under a legal duty to disclose, and
(b) intends, by failing to disclose the information—
 (i) to make a gain for himself or another, or
 (ii) to cause loss to another or to expose another to a risk of loss.

This might well catch someone who when applying for life insurance dishonestly fails to disclose that he has had a heart attack, there being a legal duty to disclose material facts when applying for insurance. Insurance contracts are unusual, however. There is no general duty to make disclosure when making contracts. Someone who recognises as a Rembrandt a picture which he is offered, is under no duty to disclose that fact to the seller. Buying it without disclosing that fact will thus not amount to fraud. Of course, if he told a lie, he might well be guilty of fraud by representation.

Fraud by abuse of position—section 4

Section 4 provides:

> (1) A person is in breach of this section if he—
>   (a) occupies a position in which he is expected to safeguard, or not to act against, the financial interests of another person,
>   (b) dishonestly abuses that position, and
>   (c) intends, by means of the abuse of that position—
>   (i) to make a gain for himself or another, or
>   (ii) to cause loss to another or to expose another to a risk of loss.
> (2) A person may be regarded as having abused his position even though his conduct consisted of an omission rather than an act.

The steward employed to work on the train or the barman in a pub who makes and sells to customers his own sandwiches, instead of those supplied by his employer, so that he can pocket for himself the takings, might well be caught by this offence.

2. OBTAINING SERVICES DISHONESTLY

Section 11 of the Fraud Act 2006 provides:

> (1) A person is guilty of an offence under this section if he obtains services for himself or another—
>   (a) by a dishonest act, and
>   (b) in breach of subsection (2).
> (2) A person obtains services in breach of this subsection if—
>   (a) they are made available on the basis that payment has been, is being or will be made for or in respect of them,

(b) he obtains them without any payment having been made for or in respect of them or without payment having been made in full, and
(c) when he obtains them, he knows—
    (i) that they are being made available on the basis described in paragraph (a), or
    (ii) that they might be,
but intends that payment will not be made, or will not be made in full.

Because of subs.(2)(a), it appears not to be an offence dishonestly to obtain a service which is supplied free. Suppose D obtains for nothing a service which would not be free if it were not for his dishonest act (e.g. a non-pensioner obtains free entry to a show by lying that he is a pensioner). It appears that here also subs.(2)(a) means that D is not guilty under s.11. Whether he might be guilty of fraud by representation depends upon whether he intends to make a "gain" or to cause or risk causing a "loss".

3. MAKING OFF WITHOUT PAYMENT

Under s.3(1) of the Theft Act 1978, if a person knows that payment on the spot is required or expected for goods or services, he commits an offence if he dishonestly makes off without paying, intending not to pay.

Mens rea

(i) The defendant must know that payment on the spot is required or expected.
(ii) He must be dishonest.
(iii) He must intend to avoid payment—and it has been held in the House of Lords that he must intend to avoid payment permanently, *Allen* (1984).

Actus reus

There is no requirement for deception. This offence is intended to catch the person who dishonestly bunks off without paying the bill.

Making off

This means leaving the actual point where payment is due, such as going past the till and into the lobby.

Authority: *Brooks and Brooks* (1983). Father and daughter had a meal in a restaurant with a third person and attempted to leave without paying. The father had passed the spot where payment should have been made but was still on the premises, near the back door. His conviction was affirmed on appeal.

Without having paid as required or expected

It is possible that the person paying with a dud cheque has "paid" for the purposes of s.3. This, however, is still an open question. Where he has paid by cheque backed with a cheque guarantee card or by credit card, then, since this guarantees that the creditor will be paid, the defendant presumably has definitely paid as required or expected. Where there is an agreement that the defendant may pay after leaving, there is no expectation that payment will be made on the spot. That is so even if that agreement was a result of deception by D.

Authority: *Vincent* (2001). D stayed at a hotel and left without paying. Charged with making off without payment, his defence was that he had discussed with the hotel proprietor as to when payment would be made and had claimed to be waiting for money that was due to him and that it had been agreed that he would pay when he could. This was held to be a good defence, even if the proprietor's agreement to postpone payment was a result of D's dishonesty.

There is no liability for making off without paying a debt which is legally unenforceable.

Authority: *Troughton v Metropolitan Police* (1987). D was a drunk passenger in a taxi, who did not tell the driver his address. The driver stopped at a police station to try to sort the matter out, and D ran off. He was charged with making off without payment, but the court held that there was no liability.

The taxi driver was in breach of contract for taking him somewhere other than his destination, and there was therefore no legal obligation on D to pay at the time he made off.

———————

11. EXAMINATION GUIDANCE QUESTIONS

1. SOME GENERAL GUIDELINES

These notes highlight matters of particular relevance in answering problem style questions in *criminal law*.

Different types of problem question

There are two broad types of criminal law examination problem. The first is characterised by a closing passage which identifies particular offences and asks the candidate to consider liability for them, e.g. "Charles has been charged under ss.20 and 47 of the Offences Against the Person Act 1861. Consider his liability, if any, on these charges." The second type does not suggest the charges at all, e.g. "Consider the criminal liability, if any, of Fred and Gert". In answering the first type of question, the candidate must deal with each of the identified charges. In the second type the candidate's first task is to identify the likely possible charges. In this case, your answer could sensibly start by listing the likely offences. A hybrid type of question might restrict the scope of the charges to be considered without identifying the precise offences, e.g. "Consider Mary's and Bill's criminal liability, if any, under the Theft Acts 1968 and 1978 and the Fraud Act 2006". This still leaves a lot of offences and again it is sensible to begin by identifying those offences (in the Theft Acts and the Fraud Act) suggested by the story.

Identify issues

Whichever the style of the question, it is worth trying to start your answer by setting out the issues to be discussed—and maybe more than just listing the likely offences. Thus, the problem story about Charles, where he is charged under s.20 and 47, may tell you that he had been drinking soft drinks which had been laced surreptitiously by his friends and also that he pushed over someone who was acting aggressively towards him. If so, it would be wise to start by stating that the issues raised *include* both self defence and also the effect of involuntary intoxication on Charles's criminal liability. The word "include" is a good one to use. It does not rule out mentioning other issues which occur to you half way through your answer.

Several parties and/or several offences

A problem may have several people in its story and it may have more than one offence to be discussed. It is generally a good idea to deal with one person at a time and one offence at a time. It is important to indicate which person and which offence is being considered. Do not be afraid to use sub-headings, e.g.: "Mary—theft", "Mary—fraud", "Bill—handling". It may even be that the same offence is possibly committed twice by the same person giving rise to sub-headings in your answer such as: "Mary—theft of kettle", "Mary—theft of handbag".

Actus reus and *mens rea*

In relation to each offence discussed, you must state whether the actor has committed the *actus reus* and whether he had the *mens rea*. As a rule of thumb it is wise to deal first with whichever is the easier to deal with in the particular problem. Imagine a murder problem which tells you "X intending to kill Y, hit him a blow causing Y to be hospitalised after which. . ." The problem may perhaps have told you a story suggesting provocation and then gone on to suggest a break in the chain of causation. One thing is clear—it has very plainly told you that X had the *mens rea* for murder. However obvious that may seem, you neverthe-less must state that he had the *mens rea* for murder and it is sensible to do so at the outset.

Defences

Whereas you must state whether the actor had the *actus reus* and *mens rea* for each crime you consider, you should deal only with *defences* which are suggested by the problem. For example, if nothing is said in the problem to suggest that X needed, or thought he needed, to defend himself (or anyone else), then do not drag the defence of self defence into your discussion of X's criminal liability.

Burden of proof

Do not mis-state the burden of proof. Generally, the burden of proof lies with the prosecution which must prove D's guilt beyond all reasonable doubt. Although there are exceptions, (e.g. in the case of insanity and, by virtue of the Homicide Act 1957, diminished responsibility, and sometimes under other statutory provisions), the general rule prevails for most of the matters to be discussed in the average criminal law examination paper. It is in relation to defences where it is easiest to get it wrong. For example, do not write "D must prove that he used no more than reasonable force to defend himself". Almost as bad is "If D proves that he used no more than reasonable force to defend himself, he is not guilty". Better to write "If D used no more than reasonable force . . .".

QUESTIONS AND ANSWER PLANS

Try answering each question, before looking at the answer plan which follows it. The answer plans are rather fuller than a student might make, but they give a general indication of the scope of an appropriate answer.

?   QUESTION 1

Bernadette volunteers to go along on a school outing as extra adult supervision is needed. She is in charge of a small group of girls. At the seaside she sunbathes while they paddle. On hearing a scream she sits up to see two girls, Elizabeth and Jane, out of their depth and drowning. She mistakenly assumes that they are playing and that there is no risk. William, a passer-by dives in and rescues the girls. Over-reacting, he gives Elizabeth unnecessary mouth to mouth resuscitation and heart massage. Unknown to him, she has a weak heart, has heart failure and dies. While all this is going on Jane is ignored and is not seen by Bernadette for several hours. She catches pneumonia due to her exposure, is ill for several months and then dies.

Discuss Bernadette's and William's criminal liability, if any, for homicide.

! ANSWER PLAN

Legal issues

Liability for Omissions, Unlawful Act Manslaughter, Manslaughter by Gross Negligence, Causation.

Bernadette

Bernadette has voluntarily undertaken responsibility, she may be liable for omitting to act. *Stone and Dobinson.* *Elizabeth's death.* She omits to act when she should. Was she grossly negligent? Was death foreseeable? Question for the jury: "Having regard to risk of death, was Bernadette's failure to act so bad in circumstances as to merit punishment as manslaughter?" *Adomako, Bateman.*

Was B's omission a substantial cause of death or was W's action an intervening act which breaks the chain? *Notman, Malcherek.* Was her omission still a significant cause despite the new act? Is victim's weak heart relevant? *Blaue.*

Does W's treatment constitute negligent medical treatment, and if so, does it make a difference? *Cheshire.*

Jane's death. Omission to care for girl. (See above).

Gross negligence, reasonable standard, foreseeability of death, *Adomako.* (See above).

Causation, operating and substantial (or significant—*Cheshire*) cause of death. (See above).

William

William's act has, apparently caused Elizabeth's death. Has he committed an unlawful act? An assault? Offences Against the Person Act 1861.—*Savage.* Dangerous? Was there an obvious risk of some physical injury, albeit minor? *Church.* William did not know of the weak heart. Would the reasonable man have known? *Dawson.* Is William's act a cause of death? *Watson, Armstrong.* Necessity. *R. v F.* Mistake regarding necessity.

Was William grossly negligent? (See above).

? QUESTION 2

Angus shows Charles how to pick a lock. He does not know exactly what Charles intends to do, although he knows he is going to "sort out" his boss, who owes him money.

Charles breaks into his boss's house and takes a painting which he estimates is of the same value as the money he is owed. He is charged with burglary and Angus is charged as a secondary party. Charles' defence is that he thought he had a right to do what he did, as he saw it as the only way of getting what he was owed. Angus's defence is that he did not know exactly what Charles would do but he thought he would simply try to get his money back.

Advise Angus and Charles as to their criminal liability, if any, and the availability of any defences.

!   **ANSWER PLAN**

Legal issues

Theft—claim of right. Burglary. Parties to crime. *Mens rea* of secondary party.

Charles

Has he committed burglary? Theft Act 1968, s.9. Section 9(1)(a) requires entry as a trespasser with intent to commit theft. What was his intent when he entered? If on entering he did not intend to commit theft, did he commit theft subsequently so as to make him guilty of burglary under s.9(1)(b)?

Defence of claim of right? Not dishonest by virtue of s.2 of 1968 Act? Did he believe he had a right in law or just a moral right? If a moral right, was he dishonest on the *Ghosh* test?

Angus

Aiding, abetting or counselling? *Att.-Gen.'s Ref. No.1 of 1975*. Did Angus commit the *actus reus* of aiding? Of counselling? *mens rea* required for secondary party. Does Angus have sufficient knowledge? How much detail does he need to know? *Bainbridge, Maxwell*. Did he know that Charles would do something illegal? If Charles is not liable, can Angus be liable as secondary party? Does Angus have to foresee just the *actus reus* of the full offence, or does he have to foresee that Charles may commit the *actus reus* with the necessary *mens rea*? *Powell, English*.

? QUESTION 3

Angus and Charles go out for a drink. Angus, knowing Charles is a diabetic, who carefully controls his drinking, spikes Charles' orange juice with vodkas. Charles, having had nothing to eat, becomes drunk very quickly and suffers a hypoglycaemic episode. During this episode he attacks and seriously injures another customer. Angus, realising that the spiked drink was the start of all the trouble, is too frightened to interfere, so hides and does nothing. Discuss the criminal liability of Charles and Angus.

! ANSWER PLAN

Legal Issues

Defences: automatism; intoxication. Assault. Sections 18, 20, Offences Against the Person Act 1861. Participation in crime. Procuring. Liability for Omissions.

Charles

Section 18, crime of specific intent. *Belfon*. Can Charles have this specific intent in these circumstances?

Section 20, 1861 Act. Grievous bodily harm (*Savage, Parmenter*) crime of basic intent.

Defences. Intoxication and its effect on liability for crimes of basic intent, different rules for crimes of specific intent. *Majewski*. Involuntary intoxication, does it make a difference? *Kingston*. Is he reckless? Possible argument based on *Hardie* would help Charles here.

Alternative defence of automatism, *Quick, Bailey*. Is it relevant that the drink is taken involuntarily and therefore automatism is not self-induced? Is *mens rea* negatived? Is there an internal or external cause here? *Hennessey*.

Angus

Is he liable as a secondary party? For aiding? For procuring? *Att.-Gen.'s Ref. No.1 of 1975. Mens rea* for secondary parties.

Blakely. If Angus is a secondary party, relevance to his liability of Charles' defence? Principal victim innocent agent? Procuring an *actus reus*? *Cogan v Leak.*

Should Angus have stepped in and prevented the violence? Is he under a duty to act due to his own prior conduct? *Miller.* What could he be liable for? Does he have *mens rea* now which he may have lacked earlier?

? QUESTION 4

Charles finds a ring on the floor of Angus's living room during a party. He puts it in his pocket, intending to find out to whom it belongs, but forgets about it. He hears the next day that it belongs to Bernadette and he tells her that he has it, offering to return it to her. She asks him to look after it for her while she is on holiday. Being short of money he pawns it, believing that he will be able to redeem it before she returns from holiday.

Later, needing to go into central London and still being short of cash, Charles takes from the desk of Henry, his flatmate, Henry's Oyster card. Henry's Oyster card, which can be used to travel on the London Underground, has £10 worth of credit on it. For his return journey, Charles realises that there is insufficient credit left on the Oyster card, so instead of "touching in" "touching out" he leaps over the barriers when entering and leaving the Underground system. Upon his return from London, he replaces the Oyster card on Henry's desk. A week later, Henry returns from his holiday with Bernadette and does not notice that the Oyster card has only £2 of credit left on it. Nor does Charles inform him.

A few days later Charles, who is a university student, finds on the ground outside his lecture hall a plasticised card containing a bar code, the words "University staff car park" and the name "Professor Bluster". The following day Charles uses the card to try to gain entrance to the staff car park where he hopes to park his car. He fails to gain admission because the entrance machine refuses the card. This is because Professor Bluster has reported the card lost and the system has been instructed not to recognise the card.

Consider which offences, if any, Charles has committed contrary to the Theft Acts 1968, 1978 and the Fraud Act 2006.

> ! **ANSWER PLAN**

Legal issues

Theft Act 1968. Appropriation. Intention of permanently depriving. Dishonesty. Fraud Act 2006. Fraud by omission. Fraud by representation. Obtaining services dishonestly. Attempting to obtain services dishonestly.
Theft Act 1978. Making off without payment.

The ring

Charles finds the ring, i.e. comes by it honestly, therefore not theft. A later assumption of the rights of an owner can be appropriation. Appropriation, s.3 of the 1968 Act. When is the moment of appropriation? *Gomez, Atakpu.* Assumption of some, or even just one, of the rights of an owner will suffice: *Morris.* Pawning is an appropriation of some rights.

Intent permanently to deprive. Parting with the property under a condition he might not be able to fulfil is deemed to be an intent permanently to deprive: s.6(2) of the 1968 Act. This covers the pawning situation. Irrelevant that he intends to redeem it and return it.

Dishonesty. Situation not covered by s.2 (1) of Theft Act 1968. Two stage *Ghosh* test: (i) is Charles dishonest by reasonable standards, and, if so, (ii) did he realise that he was? Given that he thought he could redeem the ring and intended to do so and to return it, a jury might find that he was not dishonest.

Oyster card

Theft. Charles might have stolen two things: (i) the tangible item, and (ii) intangible property comprising £8 worth of Henry's credit on the card. If he intended to inform Henry what he had done and to repay Henry, he might not have been dishonest on the *Ghosh* test (above). Equally, if he believed Henry would have agreed to him using the card had he known, then Charles could rely on s.2(1)(b) as showing absence of dishonesty. If he was dishonest, then he arguably had an intention of permanently depriving Henry of the intangible £8 worth of credit. Arguably, he should also be treated as having an intention to deprive Henry of the tangible card by virtue of having treated the thing as his own to dispose of: s.6(1) of the 1968 Act.

Fraud. By using the Oyster card, what representation has Charles made? If he has impliedly stated that he is Henry, that is a false representation. If he has done that, then the fact that he used the card by activating a machine does not stop it being a representation: s.2(5) of Fraud Act. Arguably however, he has not made that representation, since pre-paid Oyster cards are allowed to be lent to a third party. His failure to use the card on his return journey, could possibly amount to fraud by omission if he is under legal duty to "touch in" and "touch out". However, it is unlikely that he is under such a legal duty—though travelling without paying is no doubt a specific offence outside the scope of this question.

Obtaining services by a dishonest act, Fraud Act, s.11. Leaping over the barriers and thus avoiding paying is almost certainly a dishonest act. He appears to be guilty of this offence.

Staff car park card

Theft. Clearly he has appropriated it by picking it up and also by trying to use the card. Lost property is not the same as abandoned property. So, presumably it was property belonging to another, if not Professor Bluster then the university. Almost certainly dishonest on the *Ghosh* test. Not sure if Charles had the intent to deprive the owner. Perhaps he intended never to return it. If he did intend to return it sometime, it might be possible to argue that he is deemed to have the necessary intention by virtue of having treated it as his own to dispose of regardless of the other's rights or borrowed it in circumstances amounting to an outright taking: s.6(1).

Attempting to obtain services dishonestly (Criminal Attempts Act 1971 and Fraud Act, s.11). Seems not guilty if staff car parking was free (to staff): s.11(2)(a) of Fraud Act.

Fraud. If this is the relevant charge, then it is the full offence and not merely an attempt. The full offence is committed when a false representation is dishonestly made with the necessary intent. The representation is the false representation that Charles is Professor Bluster. That implied representation is made by Charles's act of presenting the card to the entrance machine: s.2(5) of the Fraud Act. There is some difficulty, however, in identifying a relevant gain or loss which Charles intended to make or cause. To be relevant it must be a gain or loss in money or other property. Without that, he is not guilty of fraud.

QUESTION 5

Charles, while drunk, breaks into a shed in someone's garden to sleep there one night. He mistakenly believes the garden belongs to a friend of his. Ursula, who is sleeping in the house, hears a noise and comes out to investigate. When she enters the shed Charles grabs her, forces her to the floor and has intercourse with her. He then pulls off rings and a bracelet she is wearing, holding her down to prevent her struggling. Afterwards he claims that because of his drunken state he mistook Ursula for his wife.

Advise Charles as to his criminal liability.

ANSWER PLAN

Legal issues

Burglary. Robbery. Theft. Sections 1, 8 and 9 of the Theft Act 1968. Rape. Trespass with intent to commit a sexual offence. Intoxication. Mistake.

Theft?

Appropriation of Ursula's jewellery? Other ingredients of the crime? Dishonesty and intention permanently to deprive? Effect of intoxication? Need for specific intent. Drunken intent or no intent to deprive permanently?

Robbery

If it is theft, does he commit robbery? Use of force before or at time of theft and in order to steal, 1968 Act, s.8.

Rape

Sexual Offences Act 2003, s.1. Irrelevant that he thought it was his wife: *R* (1992). Relevant mistake if he thought she was consenting: but only if mistake was reasonable. Evidential presumption that no reasonable mistake was made as to consent where violence was used—Sexual Offences Act 2003, s.75.

Assault, s.47 and s.20?

Holding Ursula down is a common assault? For s.47, does it occasion ABH? For s.20, holding down is not really serious injury, *Saunders*, but does the rape (if it is rape) qualify as really serious injury?

Burglary

1968 Act, s.9. Entering building as a trespasser. What constitutes a building or part of a building? Are sheds, outhouses, etc., covered? Is Charles a trespasser? Does he have *mens rea* as to being a trespasser? *Collins*. Relevance of his mistake about the owner? Relevance of intoxication? *Majewski*.

Section 9(1)(a), entry with intent (specific intent)—covers intent to commit theft, GBH. Did Charles have such an intent when he entered? Relevance of intoxication? If not guilty under s.9(1)(a), is he guilty under s.9(1)(b), having entered as a trespasser and then actually committing theft or GBH? Depends partly on answers given above. Is this version of burglary a crime of specific intent or basic intent?

Trespass with intent to commit a sexual offence

Sexual Offences Act 2003, s.63. Similar to s.9(1)(a) burglary, except that Charles has to enter (as a trespasser) with intent to commit rape (or another similar sexual offence in ss.2–4 of Sexual Offences Act). Crime of specific intent. Did he have the intent? Certain issues same as those in burglary, namely: (i) did Charles have *mens rea* as to being a trespasser? (ii) relevance to this of his intoxication—*Majewski*.

QUESTION 6

Tony and Fred are both aged 19. Tony's girlfriend is Sarah and Fred's girlfriend is Mandy. Sarah who is 15 years old looks much older than she is and the two boys believe her to be 16.

Mandy who is 16 looks younger than she is and the two boys believe her to be 15. In discussions together, each of Tony and Fred has acknowledged that he would like to have sexual intercourse with his girlfriend. In fact, each has urged the other that he should do just that. Following that conversation, they each agree that that is indeed what each will do. At no time does either boy contemplate doing anything without the consent of his girlfriend and in the boys' discussions it is understood that the sexual intercourse being discussed is to be consensual. Subsequently Tony does nothing to put the plan into action. Fred, however, does obtain Mandy's agreement to sexual intercourse, following which they get undressed and indulge in heavy sexual petting before Mandy changes her mind, with the result that sexual intercourse does not take place.

Consider whether the two boys are guilty of the following inchoate offences:

- Sexual activity with a person under 16, contrary to s.9(1) of the Sexual Offences Act 2003;
- inciting that same offence;
- conspiring to commit that same offence;
- attempting to commit that same offence.

ANSWER PLAN

Legal issues.   Inciting, conspiring and attempting to the impossible. *Mens rea* required for each inchoate offence. Whether defence available on a charge of the full offence is available in relation to charge for inchoate offence. Whether *actus reus* of full offence or of attempt committed.

Full offence.   This offence can be committed even though the victim consents. Nevertheless, this offence was not committed. The only sexual activity which took place was with Mandy, who was in fact over 16. Therefore no *actus reus* of the full offence.

Attempt.   Fred has not had sexual intercourse but he has, it seems, indulged in sexual touching of Mandy. Thus he has gone well beyond mere preparation to commit the full offence. Mandy was over 16 but on the facts as Fred believed them to be

Criminal Law

she was only 15. It appears therefore that he is guilty of attempting to commit the s.9(1) offence, as it is no defence that the crime attempted was impossible to commit: *Shivpuri*. See ss.1(2) and 1(3) of the Criminal Attempts Act 1971.

Incitement. At common law, it is not possible to be guilty of inciting the impossible: *Fitzmaurice*. Therefore Tony is not guilty at common law of inciting Fred to commit the offence in s.9(1), since Mandy is in fact over 16 and the full offence is therefore impossible. Is Fred guilty of inciting Tony to commit the s.9(1) offence with Sarah (who is under 16)? Did he have the necessary *mens rea*, an intention that the full offence be committed? Tony, if he had gone ahead, would have had a defence to charge of the full offence based on his reasonable belief that Sarah was over 16. However, the focus of incitement is on the intention of the inciter: *Claydon* (disapproving *Curr*). So did Fred have the intention that the full offence be committed?

Conspiracy—Sarah. Did Tony and Fred conspire for the commission of the offence upon Sarah? No, because no-one can be guilty of conspiracy who lacks *mens rea* (i.e. knowledge or intention) in relation to all the elements of the full offence: *Saik*. That is so even if such knowledge or intention is not required for the full offence. One of the elements of the full offence is that the victim is under 16. Neither boy knew that Sarah was under 16 and therefore neither of them is guilty of conspiracy to commit the s.9(1) offence in relation to Sarah.

Conspiracy—Mandy. Did Tony and Fred conspire for the commission of the offence upon Mandy? It appears that they are guilty, since it is an offence to conspire to commit the impossible. In this respect, the law of conspiracy is the same as the law of attempt. On the facts as believed by Tony and Fred, they agreed upon a course of action which if carried out in accordance with their intentions, would result in the commission of the full offence.

INDEX

LEGAL TAXONOMY
FROM SWEET & MAXWELL

This index has been prepared using Sweet and Maxwell's Legal Taxonomy. Main index entries conform to keywords provided by the Legal Taxonomy except where references to specific documents or non-standard terms (denoted by quotation marks) have been included. These keywords provide a means of identifying similar concepts in other Sweet & Maxwell publications and online services to which keywords from the Legal Taxonomy have been applied. Readers may find some minor differences between terms used in the text and those which appear in the index. Suggestions to *taxonomy@sweetandmaxwell.co.uk.*

(all references are to page number)

ABETTING
See Aiding and abetting
ABNORMALITY OF MIND
See Diminished responsibility
ABSOLUTE LIABILITY
See STRICT LIABILITY
ACCOMPLICES
innocent agency 29, 41–42
ACQUITTALS
principal offender 35–37
ACTUAL BODILY HARM
actus reus 85
assault 84–85
mens rea 85
offence 84–85
ACTUS REUS
actual bodily harm 85
assault 81–82
automatism 1–2
battery 83–84
burglary 136–137
causation
concurrent causes 3–4
cumulative causes 3–4
death 3
difficulties 2–3
intervening events 4–6
negligent medical treatment 6–7
result crimes 2–3

substantial cause of death 3
coincidence with *mens rea* 19–21
continuing offences 20
criminal damage 1, 139
death 3
examination guidance 151
fraud by false representation 145
grievous bodily harm 86
handling stolen goods
for the benefit of another 132–133
otherwise than in the course of the stealing 133
stolen goods 131–132
intervening events 4–6
making off without payment 148
meaning 1
mistake 61–62
murder 1, 3, 99
negligent medical treatment 6–7
omissions
contractual liability 9
law reform 10–11
positive duty 7
prior conduct of defendant 10
reform proposals 10–11
special relationships 7–9
statutory duties 10
voluntary assumption of responsibility 9
one transaction 20–21

parties 31
PROPERTY
  theft 124–126
PROVOCATION
  defence 101–107
  evidence 101–103
  loss of self control 103–104
  reasonable man test 104–106
  requirements 101
  self-induced provocation 106–107
PROXIMITY
  attempts 49, 49–50
RAPE
  consent 91, 94
REASONABLE FORCE
  self-defence 69–70
RECKLESSNESS
  "Caldwell" recklessness 16–18
  criminal damage 17–18
  "Cunningham" recklessness 15–16
  intention 12–13
  involuntary manslaughter 117
  meaning 15
  "R v G" 17–18
REFORM PROPOSALS
  See Law reform
RETAINING WRONGFUL CREDIT
  meaning 134
REVERSE BURDEN
  strict liability 26–27
ROAD TRAFFIC OFFENCES
  strict liability 25
ROBBERY
  force of fear of force 135
  immediately before or at the time
    of stealing 135
  meaning 135
SECONDARY PARTIES
  abetting 30
  acquittal of principal offender
    35–37
  aiding 30
  assisting offenders 31
  counselling 30–31
  joint enterprise 34–35
  knowledge 32–33
  mens rea 32–35
  omissions 32
  procuring 31
  repentance 37–38

types 29–30
victims 38
SELF-DEFENCE
  burden of proof 68–69
  intoxication 66–67
  law reform 79–80
  mistake 68
  reasonable force 69–71
  use of force 69–71
SEXUAL ASSAULT
  consent 91
SEXUAL OFFENCES
  assault by penetration
    consent 91
  child sex offences
    defences 93
    offences 93
  consent
    actus reus not complete 94
    assault by penetration 91
    evidence 92
    law reform 97–98
    meaning 92–93
    mistake 95–96
    mistaken belief 92
    no defence 94
    rape 91
    reasonable belief 92
    sexual assault 91
    true consent 97
  rape
    consent 91
  sexual assault
    consent 91
  Sexual Offences Act 2003 90–91
  terminology 91
  under-aged persons 93–94
SPECIAL RELATIONSHIPS
  medical treatment 7–9
  omissions 7–9
SPECIFIC INTENT
  intoxication 63, 65–66
  mens rea 15
STATUTORY DUTIES
  omissions 10
STRICT LIABILITY
  actus reus 22
  defences
    food safety offences 26
    limited form 26